MEG BR

326 SAU

408 947

374296

# Pattie Slappers

## Stories from the golden age of Hull's food processing industry

Nick Triplow

LOTTERY FUNDED

**Pattie Slappers:** researched, written and edited by Nick Triplow, Gillian Kapka and Simon King. Book design and layout by Tim Mason. Pattie Slappers © Nick Triplow 2013.

Pattie Slappers is a Community Heritage publication in association with CERT Ltd. All rights reserved. No part of this publication may be reproduced, transmitted in any form or by any means, electronic or mechanical, including photocopying, recording or any information storage or retrieval systems without prior permission.

Cover photo: Women workers at Stirk Brothers. Reproduced by kind permission of Lilian Tindle.

ISBN: 978-0-9575632-0-9

CERT Community Heritage: *www.cert-ltd.co.uk*

# CONTENTS

# Introduction – Oral History and the Pattie Slappers Project

A shortcoming of traditional history is that it tends to focus attention on the recording of momentous historical events. As a writer and researcher, this means you risk overlooking the everyday life experiences of ordinary people, those who rarely have the opportunity for their voices to be heard.

Alongside traditional historical research, Pattie Slappers brings together the words, stories and memories of those who lived through the good times and years of decline of Hull's food processing industry. Oral history recognises that memories are a mixture of fact and opinion. They are, by their nature, selective or can become hazy over time and, of course, people may be influenced by stories heard or read later. Where possible, events in this book are cross-referenced and verified.

Oral history should delve deeper than generic folk memory: the truth, as always, is in the detail and I'm grateful to those who came forward, told us their stories and gave such a vivid and realistic appreciation of a way of life. The interviews collected in Pattie Slappers have given people an opportunity to make sense of their own experiences. Bringing them together under one cover recognises and values their wider contribution to the city's history.

As for the legendary Pattie Slappers themselves, there's no doubt they could make the factory floor an intimidating workplace. When I interviewed Philip Harmer, the last manufacturing manager at Hull's Birds Eye factory, I asked had he ever sent a young manager down to the production lines knowing the women would have him for breakfast? He laughed, 'Yeah, every day.'

**Nick Triplow**
**February 2013**

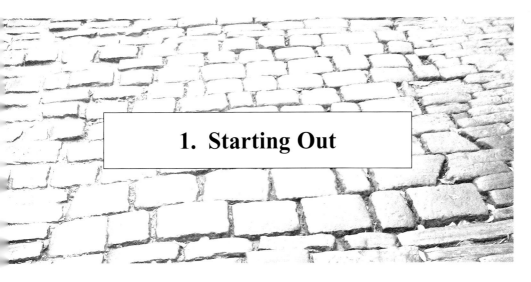

# 1. Starting Out

*'I said, "Look, I can't get me hands round the bloody thing."'*

For many women, their entry to the fish processing industry came from a sudden or temporary need. A shortage of cash, clothes for the kids and in extreme cases, the loss of a husband or father at sea. In years gone by, the flexibility demanded of women bringing up families and the need to provide a regular income had largely depended on established crafts such as net-braiding. Hessle Road historian Alec Gill has written about women braiding nets 'in practically every street of Hull's fishing community, especially between Strickland Street and Gillett Street'.

Net braiding may have been poorly paid, but it could be accomplished at home and at times of the day which enabled women to look after their children. With the advent of post-war mass production and new food processing techniques, similar flexible working patterns would become commonplace in the short shifts and part time opportunities of the food processing companies.

In a very real sense, traditional fish house workers were 'good time girls', living and working with the fatalism of fishermen; men who lived with the knowledge that 'if the sea wants yer, it'll take yer.' The women swore, they sang when the mood took them, they looked after their own and were suspicious of outsiders. But most of all, they worked.

In the early 1960s, Margaret Green came into the industry. Like many mothers she needed extra cash in the run up to Christmas.

'I was about twenty and the kids were only little. I worked down Rutters on West Dock Avenue. I needed toys for 'em for Christmas. A girl that lived near my mum, who I'd known from being young, she worked there with her mother, Nora, and she said, "We can get you a job there Margaret, at the pattie place."'

Margaret wasn't exactly thrilled at the idea, but took the job. With her mum looking after the children, she was able to work full time. Later she worked at Kaywoods, once again earning money for her children.

'I was talking to this woman – we did salt cod – y'know it went to Africa, and I said, "What do they call you?" And she said, "Annie, Annie Bird." I said, "Are you married?" She said, "Yeah, they call me 'usband Dicky." Well I fell off the stool. The first day!

'This Mrs Bird, she was posh, from Anlaby. I used to say, "What are you doin' down Hessle Road?" Her 'usband used to come and pick her up in this big car. And she used to tek her overall off, put her make up on and she must've gone home and the neighbours would never have known where she worked.'

Workers at Birds Eye stacking cod in parsley sauce ready for freezing circa 1980s

In 1968, Pearl Anderson also found herself needing to bring in some extra money for Christmas. Along with her sister, she went to work in a fish house.

'It was horrible and noisy; everything was wet. The women used to break cod heads off with their hands. And they put me on that, heading. It's a knack. You had the cod – it'd be about three foot long – and you'd give it a twist and break its neck backwards and it'd come off. You didn't cut it off, it was broke off. It was an 'orrible job. I couldn't do it. Compared to the people that was working there my hands were small and they're not strong.

'My sister, who's smaller than me, she was working by the side and she looked at me and I looked at her … I just put my hand up and said, "I can't do this." He (the supervisor) said, "Try." I said, "Look, I can't get me hands round the bloody thing." So he took me to a sluice room where all the rubbish was and said, "Clean that." And I loved it. Me sister got put cleaning somewhere else. I don't like cleaning at the best of times but anything was better than that.

'They (the women in the fish houses) were ordinary people, but they'd always done that kind of work. I'd never done a job like that. I'd never touched wet fish unless me father'd said, "Take this to your mother." It was the first time I'd ever worked in a fish house, because in my family they used to say, "You'll end up in a fish house." I'd say, "I won't, I won't." That was the worst place to work. It was cold and hard and it smelled. And they weren't nice girls in fish houses. It was hard work and they was hard women. But when you went to work at Birds Eye, they was posh. You had a uniform, you didn't go in your own clothes. The women used to get made up, you'd think they was going out. They used to do their hair, used to have their rollers under their turban, with a roller out the front.'

In the post war period there were plenty of opportunities for school leavers to earn decent money on the fish docks, especially if you were willing to work hard, learned quickly and could handle the physical demands of being a barrow lad. Like many boys leaving West Dock Avenue School – the 'barrow lads college' – John Talbot knew his options would be limited. He'd already been to sea on a pleasure trip with skipper Frank Rasmussen, a mate of his dad's, but John's mother refused to allow her son to go to sea. 'What put the tin 'at on it was two trips after that Frank got killed on that same ship I'd been on.'

When, in April 1947, the post-war Labour Government raised the school leaving age from 14 to 15, John thought he'd have to stay 'another year in jail'. But he left school in the summer holidays a few weeks before his fifteenth birthday.

'I left on the Friday at four o'clock and I walked on the fish dock and got a job. I had a place to go to, someone said go to this firm, Pickles, as they wanted a barrow lad. So I walked the full length of the market. As I was walking down, it was still busy. They were saying, "Just left school son, do you wanna job?" I started work on the Monday.

'When you first start as a barrow lad, you were to follow your boss up. There was two of us on, two lads and him. At first they used to let you bring one kit back at a time, but after a couple of days you had to learn to get two. In the first week I was still taking them one at a time, then I had to try and get two kits on. I lifted 'em up see and I couldn't do it, I had to put the barrow down. I couldn't get it and me barrow kept slipping away and this bloke, Albert Baxter, he'd be in his twenties, he said, "Oh I'll do it." And he just picks it up and puts it on the barrow. I thought, I'll never be as strong as that.'

The barrows the lads used could carry anything up to 40 or 50 stone from the market to the merchants stands and the trains. John learned to handle the weight. Albert Baxter would go on to set up Baxters Transport. But for the time being, the fourteen year old John Talbot was simply happy to be working and earning.

'Three pound a week was my first wages. And I had two shillings stopped, don't know what for. Just two shillings stopped. So I got two pound eighteen shillings. I was quite pleased. Me mam says, "You shouldn't have nothing stopped." My mam was good to me she didn't take nowt.'

Eddie Rokahr left school at fifteen in 1959. In a community where almost everybody was connected to the fishing industry, he too started work on the fish market.

'My local school was right on top of the fish docks. I left on the Thursday before Good Friday and started work on the Tuesday after Easter Monday. I started off as a barrow lad like everybody else and spent about three and a half years down there.'

Bob Carlson had wanted to work on the docks. At the age of fourteen he had his chance, but didn't last long.

'At the end of the dock there used to be a box pool with all these six-stone wooden boxes. If anybody wanted a barrow lad, they'd go to the box pool and say, there's a job for you. And you got put down the market, and that's how I got a start. But I messed up really, because the first day I went I was cheeky and this bloke said, "We can't be doing with people like you, but I've got a job for you." And he put me in a fish house. I didn't want to be in a fish house. When you were fourteen you wanted to be with the lads on the dock. So that was my punishment. I got stuck in the fish house till I was sixteen.'

Philip Bunting earned himself the nickname 'Prince Philip' with the women at East Yorkshire Fish Products in 1969. The factory had a rivalry with the nearby Kingston Fishcakes. Philip made a start 'spud bashing'.

'Dora was the gaffer, not officially but she was in charge. You could 'ave a bit of fun, but if she was mad at yer, she was mad at yer. I started spud bashing, peeling the tatties and tipping 'em into a big rack so the women could sort 'em out, pick all the eyes out, stones out. They'd put 'em on trays and put 'em in ovens to steam 'em. For a few months, that's all I did all day. Then I got promoted into cooking the fish – that meant putting the fish in to trays and taking 'em in the oven to cook.'

Philip was a fresh-faced 17 year old when he learned not to cheek the women on the production line and received his 'induction'.

'They did all sorts to me. They put a hose pipe down me back and neck and turned it on. The women where they used to make wooden boxes for the fish cakes, you didn't upset them; they had rubber stamps to put on the boxes. And one day I went in having a laugh and a joke and they says, "We'll get you ya little bugger." One day they did: pants down and rubber stamped I was, with little red rings all over. It did come off – eventually.'

He remembers another new lad who came off worse in the packing room.

'They 'ad like a big wooden bench goin' along. They used these pressure guns and staplers to staple the box lids, then pass 'em on. We 'ad a lad who was a bit lippy, he got a bit gobby to the women. So I sent 'im in there and they grabbed 'im, laid 'im on this wooden bench and stapled all of 'is clothes. And he was goin', "You bastard, you bastard."'

Karen Rouse-Dean was still at school when she worked part-time in a Hessle Road greengrocers. Wanting to stay on at school and of working age, Karen needed to earn her keep and in the summer holidays took a job at McCrae's in Gloucester Street.

'They did kipper fillets. They told me I wouldn't get paid 'til the following week, said I had to work a week in hand. When I went home I said to me mam, "What does that mean?" She said, "You don't get paid this week, you get paid next week for this week's work." So when they all got paid out on the Friday, they give me a wage packet. And I thought, well this is weird they told me I was working a week in hand. When I opened the envelope, it was just fish eyes with a little note to say, "To see you through to next week."'

Marion Carlson started work at Eskimo Foods, Strickland Street in 1966. The company changed names and ownership over the years, but the work stayed the same.

'That was fish. There was skinning machines, there was men that was gullying, y'know, gutting all the inside out. My first job was V-boning. You get a slice of fish and you have to V-bone it out. They showed you how to do it, but when you'd first left school you weren't sure, but you soon go into it.'

Later Marion would work for Finbar and Birds Eye.

Workers at Birds Eye stacking cod in parsley sauce ready for freezing circa 1980s

'Going into work it was like they were your sisters, you'd help each other. Say somebody hadn't got nowt for breakfast, they'd 'elp yer. If somebody's finding the job hard, they'd 'elp yer. They was true friends.'

Like many women, Ivy Gallagher's first job at Birds Eye was on a production line sorting fish for quality.

'I worked on what they called troweling. They had these massive trays and when they had mushed all the fish an' that together they put them on this tray and you had to trowel it. I'm real good at plastering walls because of that job.

'When I was at Birds Eye the first time my husband was in the army. I thought I'd go get a job and I told the woman next door I was starting work. I said, "Will you look after the bairn on a night?" I used to put her to bed in my house, but next door she used to listen out for me coming home. People these days think that they are hard done to but when you think about what we went through to put bread on the table it really was hard. I missed out on my children's childhood because I had to work, but I wouldn't swap it. I enjoyed what I did. You mixed in, you got to know people you would never have known. I was only seventeen an half when I got married. I enjoyed my life doing that and I learnt a lot of things. I can do a lot that I couldn't have done otherwise.'

Unlike the majority of the dock and fish processing workers, the Galloways came from east Hull. John Galloway had started work for Jeff Fields, an established fish merchant, before the war. Apart from wartime service in the Royal Navy – the market had closed and operated from the north west coastal town of Fleetwood for the duration – John worked on the docks until he retired. Leaving school in 1952, John's younger brother, Mike, worked at the Co-op until John suggested he find a job on the docks. Mike followed his brother into the industry in 1953, starting out as a barrow lad.

'They saw a bit of potential in me so I got a job on the fish dock in the little box office. There was loads and loads of small fish merchants – must've been the best part of 200 on the dock. There was two markets. Our stand was one-three-nine and we were roughly halfway along the Icelandic market. Then there was the North Sea market prior to us. There were big and small; some were just two or three men – maybe a filleter, someone taking the orders and a barrow lad.'

After a job at Frank Dees and a period on government schemes, Lorraine Scott followed her mother Lilian, then at Birds Eye, into the fish and food processing industry, packing fish by hand at McConnachies when she was 17.

'I couldn't stand the smell of it. It was 'orrible. You stunk, could never get the smell off yer. There was a smokehouse just round the corner and we used to pack that as well, mackerel and kippers. Sometimes you'd have to take the little white worms out. There was little white worms in it. It really was horrible. I don't eat fish now. Don't eat it at all. My dad used to go to sea on the standby boats and he used to do his own rod and lining. If he brought fish home that he'd caught, I'd eat it. But if me dad hadn't caught it I wouldn't eat it after what I'd seen in the fish house.'

Lilian Scott's Birds Eye career began with a season sprout trimming. As the season came to an end, Lilian took time away from work to look after one of her children.

'When I come back one of the girls I'd started with said, "Oh, I've put your name down for fish." So I says, "Thanks, I don't wanna work with fish." She says, "Oh well I've put your name down. I said you'd work." So I ended up giving it a try.'

Now in her 91st year, Jose Verbist had intended to work at Birds Eye for a season. With her husband in the RAF often away on detachment, and her children growing up, Jose took the opportunity to go looking for work.

'I went on my bicycle up Boothferry Road and through Riverside, where Birds Eye used to be. I thought I'd be there about three months and I was there twelve years. I just thought it'd be a little job so I wouldn't be too lonely. And I'm not the sort of person who wants to be sitting indoors all the time.

'When I first went there, they looked at me, y'know, asked where I'd come from. I said, "Well originally I'm from Dartford, Kent." They said, "You're not one of us, you shouldn't be here. You're a foreigner, taking one of our jobs away." I said, "We're all foreigners. In England there's more foreigners than anywhere else in the world." After a while we all got on pretty well. I think we did, I mean, I am one of them and this is my home, that's how I look on it.'

Workers at Summit Fish Products loading trays 1959

As a 21 year-old, Beatty Lee was renting two rooms in a terraced house. Knowing Beatty was in need of a job, her landlady who had recently started work at Humberside Food Products at the bottom of West Dock Avenue, suggested she apply for a job there. Her stay was short, but memorable. In the mid-1950s Humberside Foods were trading under the brand name 'Summit'.

'It said Summit on the crisps and Summit on the patties, but it was called Humberside Food Products when I worked there, which made it sound very nice but it was pretty Dickensian. I needed stamps because I was pregnant and you needed them to get maternity allowance, so I went for four weeks to top up the stamps. Much as it was horrific I went back the next year because I wanted a new coat and a frock for Christmas and I didn't have no money. I went back for another month, but it was like I'd been there for a year. They didn't give us a target, but we worked absolutely nonstop. There wasn't time to breathe. It was very, very hard work. The only good thing about Humberside Food Products was that it wasn't wet, because they often are when its fish. It wasn't pleasant. I didn't even get to know anybody. I went to work and that's all I did.'

A Hessle Roader born and bred, Patricia Rudd had worked on farms 'tattie-pulling' and bean-picking at the age of twelve and thirteen. It meant standing in a field in all weathers, bent over, for a shilling a day. She left school on a Friday and started work at Birds Eye the following Monday on £3 a week. 'Me father said, "Go get a job."' At the age of fourteen, Patricia found the shifts hard going.

'You were brought up hard and you was working hard. I was on from six to two, two to six, and ten until six on a night. So you did three shifts. A week of one lot then you changed, do another shift, another time and the next week you changed back to another time so was in a circle all the time. It was 'ard trying to catch up with yer sleep, it was all odd, because it was different shifts. You'd do overtime Saturday and Sunday.

'When I first started there was me and another girl on this line by ourselves and we had a box of fish each. He (the supervisor) showed us what to do and said, "I want you to do them and let me know when you've finished." I starts and cuts this fish up and I said, "Done this one." This other girl's only half way through. He said, "Well wait a minute then." And he takes it away and he comes back and says, "Can you do another one?" I said, "Alright." I does another one and this lass next to me says, "Can you slow down a bit?" So I says, "Well I can't." Your hands were freezing, you couldn't feel your fingers 'cos when the fish had been filleted, they'd put the slices in ice cold water, then it used to go in the freezers, then it would come out on a pallet and you 'ad to take a box and V-bone it, but your 'ands were that cold. And the times you'd cut yourselves and someone would say to yer, "You're bleeding." You 'ad no feeling in yer fingers 'cos it was so cold.

'I'd only done these couple of boxes and the supervisor says to me, "Have you done this before?" I says, "No." So he says, "Come with me." And he put me on this line with all these women. Well the women didn't like it. They was frightened they wasn't goin' to get their bonus. They thought I'd be slow because I was new and I was young. I mean I was only four foot five when I left school at fourteen. And they thought I was too young and shouldn't be on that line 'cos they was experienced women.

'They didn't know that me dad 'ad a fishing boat and he used to take us out fishing and he used to have crab pots. And we used to go crabbin', put fish 'eads in the crab pots and go tek 'em out, y'know. I was used to handling stuff from being a bain. That's how I come to be quick. Because me dad always taught us to do everything. I mean there was seven of us, so we 'ad to learn from being little.'

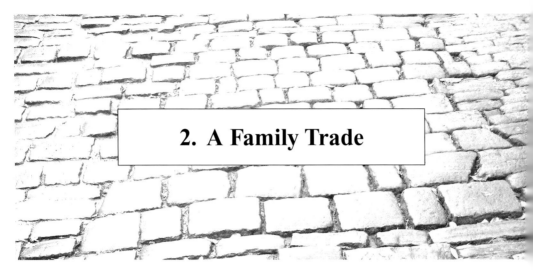

# 2. A Family Trade

*'It was like that when I was young, you worked in the fish house you was the lowest of the low.'*

For as long as she could remember, Janet Wilson's family had lived in the Hessle Road area. Like many men, when her father, Alf Anderson, came out of the army, he found work as a bobber on the fish docks. At the time the family were living with Janet's grandmother in a small house in Havelock Street.

'My auntie lived at the first house, I was born at the second, me uncle had the shop at the third, me other auntie lived at the fourth. That's how it was: everybody lived together. Later we moved to Bricknell Avenue, but didn't stay. It was a long way for me dad to walk to the docks in the morning and it unsettled me mam. We moved back down Somerset Street – me dad was at Brekkes. My memories of him going to work was hearing him walking up the passage early in the morning – you had a long passage at the side of your house, to get in the back way. You had to go the back way 'cos your clothes stunk. All you could hear was his clogs echoing under the alleyway and disappearing into the distance. Me mam used to wait for him coming back, listen for his clogs coming.'

Bobbing was a much sought after job and family connections were useful. A short time after his father died in 1955, John Talbot went into the trade, at first as a casual worker.

'You had to get a job and work your way up. When I first started, the boss didn't know me. He set all these other people on, just standing there, askin' their names. It was right medieval really. And then he'd say, "That's it." He'd walk away. You wouldn't get a job and you wouldn't get paid. Luckily there was a lot of ships so he wanted more blokes and he says to me, "What's your name?" I says, "Talbot." And he looked straight at us, that's all he did. So he sent me to the ship and about three in the morning he come down and he says, "Are you Jack's lad?" I says, "Yeah." Next day I was on the list, so he called me name out.'

Listening for the clicks of bobbers' clog irons in the street was a twice-daily event. Commonly worn by dock workers, made locally at places like Walsh's on Dairycoates and re-ironed periodically, the clogs would keep feet dry and give a firm footing on the slippery dockside. Janet Wilson's father would eventually leave his clogs behind and move into the industry, becoming a factory manager. He would often take Janet and her brother into work with him on a Sunday 'to check on things'.

'We'd have our Sunday best clothes on, but he used to open the freezer doors and have us climbing over the fish. There was a whale in there once that he took us to see. Just climbing over this great big whale, it filled the cold store. They caught anything then, it didn't seem to matter.'

Janet would work for Ross's in the Brighton Street factory canteen 'not getting her hands dirty' according to her friend Pearl Anderson. Janet's dad was Pearl's boss. Pearl's family also lived close together in the heart of the fishing community. Their Liverpool Street houses were owned by the same landlord, their exteriors painted a distinctive maroon colour.

Workers at Brekkes, Alf Anderson standing circa 1970s

'If somebody moved out, someone always had a daughter or a son that was getting married or just got married, or living with their granny in the front room. So as soon as somebody died usually, you'd move in. I had an aunt living at number one, my grandmother at number three, another aunt at number eight, another at number ten and her daughter lived at number eleven. Another aunt lived at fourteen and we lived at number fifteen, right opposite the docks.

'We'd go over the train lines, over the bridge, and tell the copper me dad's ship was coming in. He'd ask what ship was he on, look it up and say, "No, he won't be in yet, come back in two hours." And then he'd let us go through all the men working and onto the dock and they'd chuck us on the ship, from one man to another.'

One day a week, Pearl's mother would rent a twin-tub washing machine. It was a revelation, far removed from the posher and dolly tub that had served the fishing communities for years.

'The bloke used to bring it and purrit in the back yard, charge her two bob for the day. People used to come out the woodwork. It'd be, "Pearl, would you just put us this through," or "Pearl, would you just put us that through". And at the end of the day she had no idea whose washing it was, ours or theirs. And then the bloke'd come back and the conditions were it had to be as clean as when he'd brought it. Some people paid one shilling and threepence to have it for half a day. Then he'd go onto someone else for another half a day and make an extra sixpence.'

For most houses without baths or showers, keeping clean involved a series of time-consuming weekly chores. Women faced a huge challenge to wash and dry clothes in the days before household appliances. Ivy Gallagher's Friday morning trip to the St Paul's Street wash house was typical, an experience shared by many and essential for a fish house worker.

'We lived in a two-up, two-down and I used to wear my overall to go home in sometimes and we'd hang them outside in what we called the coal house. You never got rid of the smell from your skin. You could see people sat on the bus could smell fish. It didn't matter how much perfume you put on or how many times you got washed, you never ever got rid of that smell. When we came home we'd get washed in a bowl, go to bed and it would get on your bedding but you can't smell it yourself. Everything you touched was fish.

'I used to go to the wash house every Friday morning down St Paul's Street. I remember walking through the doors, paying, and on one side there were all the scrubbing stalls for things you don't put in machines. They had a sink and a draining board and you had a dolly tub and dolly stick and you did all your things in there. At the back they had these massive drums and in the middle was a big lid you lifted up and put whites in there. You took them out of there and put them in the spinners. They had big airers that you could pull out and hang your clothes on. Then you took them off there into another room where they had big ringers that you had to put tuppence in and they used to mangle everything instead of ironing everything. It used to pop all the buttons off my husband's shirts.

'We had a wash house pram that we used take the clothes in for a six o'clock in the morning boil. My husband used to go to work at eight-thirty, so I had to get it done and get home before he went to work. You had to book the day before to get in for the Friday. Then at Christmas you had to go at four in the morning to stand in the queue to book a wash for the next day. It felt horrible having to do it but you just had to. No one else is going to do it for you are they?'

With extended families often living close together, it would become the norm for fathers to work with sons, mothers with daughters. Lorraine Scott went into the processing industry at Birds Eye knowing she had her mum, her aunt and her sisters Joanne and Andrea already working in the factory.

'Then me nephew went there and then me brother-in-law. It was all families. And then there was quite big families. And then you was thinking, I didn't know they was relations; they could be sisters y'know what I mean. But everybody got on with each other. There wasn't a lot of bitchiness. As soon as I went and they'd say, "Oh you're Lil Scott's daughter, you can come and work on our line." If they didn't know yer they'd be like, "I don't like the look of that one." You 'ad to prove yourself. We got on with everybody because we was a biggish family.'

As Manufacturing Manager for Birds Eye No.1 Building in Hull, Philip Harmer was in charge of fish processing operations. He had been an engineer and found himself responsible for the work of 700 people. He recognised the importance of the family atmosphere, all part of the Birds Eye ethos.

'It was very labour intensive even in recent years. Predominantly the women worked part-time shifts designed around their work styles and children. So there were five hour shifts, which were popular because they could get baby sitters for five hours. Once you get beyond that you get in to all sorts of problems. I thought they brought a family atmosphere and a social dimension to the factories which would otherwise have been missing.'

For many families in the heart of the fishing community, the threat of a loss at sea was never far away. The knock-on effects would be felt throughout the community. For Eddie Rokahr, like numerous others, the dangers of the fishing industry were to shape his life.

'Me grandfather was fishing, me dad was fishing, all his brothers were fishing. The fellow I'm named after, my dad's brother, he was lost off the Faroe Islands in 1931. Me granddad, he was seconded from the fishing fleets to the Naval minesweepers and their boat was rammed unfortunately by a Royal Naval ship, so my grandfather went down with his ship. After the war me dad went back fishing and he was on the winch and the warp snapped and took his 'and off. Six weeks later me dad was dead. And that's when I said, "If they want fish and chips, they'll make do with chips." I was five year old.'

The men in Marion Carlson's family were also fishermen. They were no strangers to the unforgiving nature of the sea.

'Me dad was a fisherman. Me uncle – me mum's brother – he picked the mine up what blew up. He was in the St Hubert. I lost me uncle – me dad's brother – in the Rodrigo and me mam's uncles, Sid Ness and Arthur Ness, they was skippers. A lot of the women I worked with in the fish houses, their husbands were fishermen. They didn't have a lot of money and if they were in debt, we used to help 'em out. If a ship went over, the women'd get together. If anybody was late for work, you'd clock 'em on. So they didn't lose nowt.'

Ivy Gallagher lived with her grandmother opposite a smokehouse in Witty Street. Ivy would watch as the girls hung the kippers on rods and passed them in to smoke.

'It would have been around 1949. My aunties and my mam used to work at these fish houses. When I was about seven or eight my Mam used to fetch kippers home in tracing paper – that's what they wrapped them up in. She did that on a night and braided fish nets in the day.

'In the living room where the stairs was she had two hooks. When it was raining, that's where she braided. We used to thread the needles for her and when the sun was shining she'd take it outside. She'd have spent quite a few hours in the day doing the nets and a six-to-ten shift on a night. My dad was killed before I was born but my stepfather, he went big-boating so mam had to do it to keep us.'

Ivy's stepfather was away for up to a year at a time on the 'big boats', leaving her mother with no choice but to leave Ivy, her sister and brother on their own at night while she went to work.

'I'd have been about six or seven year old, my brother was eight or nine. My brother was in charge. We had an accident one night when she was at work. We used to play ball, throwing it down the stairs and me sister forgot to let go and fell down the stairs.'

John Talbot's family had strong connections to the fishing industry. His grandfather had been the lock gateman, bringing ships in and out of the fish docks. His grandmother would tell stories of how they coped in poorer times.

'Before the war when there was still plenty of fish, but people had even less money, they used to buy the cod heads for a penny. They'd boil 'em up and cut the cod cheeks out – there's plenty of fish in the cod cheeks. They'd boil 'em up and make jelly, brine, y'know. Nowadays if they cooked it on telly it'd be a delicacy, but me gran was doing it years ago.

'We lived right opposite Barchard's wood yard on West Dock Street, so we used to climb over and pinch the logs on a night time. Though things were cheaper then, people were skint.'

Tales of pawn shops and suits or wedding rings pledged for a few shillings as soon as fishermen left for sea are legend in fishing communities. Janet Wilson remembers a more unusual pledge.

'They used to pawn dishes of bread dough. Their houses were so cold and the pawn shop was so warm that they'd put it in there so it'd rise nice. And then go back a few hours later and pay a ha'penny or whatever and get the bread back. Their houses were too cold and damp for the bread to rise.'

With many families experiencing levels of poverty that made day-to-day living a constant struggle, friends and neighbours often provided the lifeline to support those in need. Pearl Anderson remembers the story of a young mother in Liverpool Street in 1958, not long after her brother had been born.

'This woman had just had her baby. She sent her lad round to sell us a tin of National Health milk. Me father said, "Yeah, buy it." So we put it in the cupboard. My brother couldn't drink national health milk, he could only drink Ostermilk. A few hours later there was another knock at the door. Me father said, "Get that National Health milk." It was the woman's lad again. He said, "Can mam have some food for the baby?" She'd sold it to us to buy food for the younger ones, then needed the milk for the baby. My father knew she'd come back for it, but pride wouldn't let her just take the money. Her husband left her virtually destitute. He come home and he was dressed to the nines, she never went out, house full of kids.'

Jane Rudd gave birth to nine girls in ten years, two of whom died. 'You used to have children quick in them days.' Her second daughter, Patricia, grew up as one of seven sisters in a two-up, two-down. As soon as they were old enough, the children went out to work.

'That's what you did, you left school, you got a job but you didn't open your pay packet, it went straight to yer mam and then she'd give you money for your dinner every day.'

Jane's eldest daughter, Patricia's sister, was reluctant to take a job in a fish house, preferring to work in an office. Patricia remembers them walking in the street.

'She wouldn't walk on same side of street as me, because I worked in the factory and she worked in the office. Honest to God, we was walking down the street. I was on that side of the road and she was on the other side and she wouldn't let me walk with her because she worked in the office. She was learning to be a wages clerk and I worked in the factory you see.'

It didn't bother Patricia, who was earning a living and paying her way, but as their mother remembers, her eldest wasn't the only one to look down on the factory girls. Particularly before the war, the street you lived in and the way you earned a living was an important signifier of social status.

'It was like that when I was young, you worked in the fish house you was the lowest of the low. I only worked for a little while in the fish house itself doing what Pat did, 'cos I had a family and the family was growing up. My dad worked in a cod farm, where they smoked the cod and the haddock, and because my dad worked in a smoke house, I worked in a little wooden shack making cups of tea and bramble pies for the workers. I used to go in, make their morning cup of tea, then I'd go out along the dock, collect brambles, take 'em back, wash 'em and take 'em home that day, bake, and then bring the pies back next day. That's what life was like. Never stopped working 'til two year ago, even if it was voluntary the last few years.

'If you lived on one side of Hessle Road, Liverpool Street and Brighton Street, you were on the poor side. We had family that lived down Westbourne Street area and they'd walk past you in the street. That was the posher area even though it was Hessle Road. There was a divide. I think it was because most of them women on that side, Liverpool Street side – that's where I was brought up – they worked on the docks and in the fish houses, whereas the others worked in shops or in other factories. In the bakeries, Jackson's and that sort. They were still working, but they had better jobs, cleaner jobs let's put it that way.

'It was strange for us because my dad's family, his cousins and all that, we never met up with them. I only met up with one of them about a year ago for the first time. She was doing a family tree and she contacted me and said, wasn't it strange that we'd never met before. I went to school with two of my cousins and yet they didn't talk to me. I wasn't posh enough. It was accepted that we socialised with the people we lived with and they socialised with theirs. Even if it was family.'

Jane remembers the Second World War as the unifying influence, the point at which people came together. 'From my point of view, after that in the forties and fifties people did mingle more. People did stick together.'

One notable Hull firm at the retail end of the fishing industry has made a virtue of its family ties. Bob Carver's distinctive presence at Hull Fair and in the family-run fish and chip shop dates back to the beginning of the 20th century. Bob is now in his 60s and still frying.

'We've always been a family firm. Me grandfather started off with a stall in the market, him and his brothers. And then me nan, his wife, she came into the business. They was in the market for seventy or eighty years. We've been here (Trinity Wharf) for thirty-three years. I'm the third generation and I've never thought of doing anything else, I don't know anything else. I was brought up into it by me dad. I used to do the chips. We had a little warehouse in Mytongate and that's what I started doing when I was a kid, fifty three years ago.'

Although his brothers took a different path, Bob's wife, Carol, and daughter, Jade, have come into the family business and his son has another shop in Chapel Street. 'It used to be me and me son, but now I've got this one, he's got that one.'
    In an article for the Hull Fair website, Bob spoke about Bob Carver's on the fair before the war.

'We used to be on the ground with a big sit-down tent with about twenty waitresses. It wasn't seats it was more like tables and trestles with white table cloths. It all had to be moved at the end of the fair so we had something easy to set up and take down. In the early days we used to do fish on the fair but when we moved onto the roadway we didn't do the fish because we only had coke fires … So since the war we've always done pattie, chips and peas.'

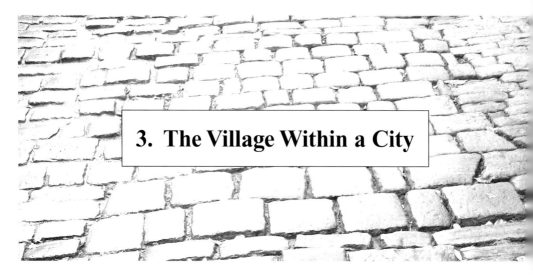

# 3. The Village Within a City

*'We'd run in like 'ell, get half a lager, packet of crisps and back to work.'*

The lives of people working on the docks and in fish houses and factories were dependant on a mixture of family, extended family and informal neighbourhood networks. From the workplaces to the shops, streets, pubs and clubs in and around Hessle Road, the 'village within a city' forged an identity founded on deep-rooted traditions of the fishing industry and a shared sense of hardship.

John Talbot's memories of Hessle Road date back to the Second World War. As a small boy, knowing no different, the blitz became another kind of 'normal'. He was four when his father went away to fight in Burma and nine when he came back.

> 'When the air raids first started we went in the fish houses, down the mush holes where they kept all the sawdust. So you were in the mush hole, right in the cellars under the fish houses, all the old ladies with their tins with insurance books. That's all they had, insurance books, birth certificates and a little bit of jewellery. That was their possessions. In the air raid shelter everybody sat in the same place it seemed, so you were all sat there, Talbots 'ere, the Matsons there, Wilsons there.'

A fisherman coming home would invariably bring a bass of fish to share with family, friends and neighbours. As Eddie Rokahr says, 'it was a free meal'. Local fish and chip shops would fry the fish for you, 'as long as you bought a bag of chips'.

> 'We used to get free school meals 'cos we had no father. And I'm not ashamed of the fact 'cos I wasn't on me own. Virtually every kid on 'essle Road at some time or another lost a member of family to the fishing – 'alf the kids off 'essle Road, right through for generations, had one parent families because they'd only their mother to bring 'em up: the fathers were away three weeks at a time

fishing. They were nothing but one parent families. That's what made it a community.'

For communities to remain closely-knit depended on daily acts of kindness and consideration. In the days before meals on wheels, Beatty Lee's mother would send a dinner into their elderly and unwell next-door neighbours and, as Beatty remembers, her own neighbours helped her out.

'I lived in Marmaduke Street when I had my little girl. I went in there two days before she was born and one woman used to get up at six o'clock and sweep the whole terrace from the bottom. Then another lady used to come out and do all the windows and another lady used to come out and donkey-stone your

Rosamund Street, Hessle Road 1975

step. They'd do it for you all the time: once you lived down there one person was designated to doing it. When I had my little girl, if she was out on the front they used to just open the door and say, "I'm taking her over road, Beatty." And they used to take them up Hessle Road with them to do their shopping. When I re-married and lived in Gypsyville and used to put the bairns on the front nobody ever used to help. Things had altered by that time – the start of keeping up with the Joneses.'

There was also help on hand for the significant events of life and death. As Beatty remembers, 'You could always run down the street and get someone.' Margaret Green's grandmother was a terrace midwife. The tales of these older, more experienced women entered folklore.

'They used to call my granny Mrs Fetch 'em and stretch 'em. She had a beige bag for delivering babies and a grey bag for laying people out and washing them. She was ninety-odd when she died, a lovely old lass. Used to do net braiding. I'd fill the needles till me fingers was sore. She used to say, "If you fill the needles today, I'll make you a knotted swing for the lamp-post." How we didn't kill ourselves swinging round I do not know.'

In the middle of the community were the pubs and clubs. A fishermen who was broke or out of a ship need only to stand outside Rayners at 11 o'clock for a handout from others coming off the docks with money in their pockets. Bob Carlson remembers fishermen helping each other out, 'They called it hovelling.'

Marion Carlson's grandparents, Charlotte and Harry Ness, had run Millers pub on the corner of Hawthorn Avenue. Marion and her brother were born there and spent much of their childhood in the pub's upstairs flat.

> 'I'd go down to me granddad to get some crisps and they used to have a little old snug as you come down the stairs, and there were these little old women in black clothes drinking from a jug.'

Charlotte Ness had the measure of the fishermen who drank in Millers. As Marion remembers, she was 'very strict' and would stand for no nonsense. Charlotte and Harry's son George was a skipper whose ship, the St Hubert, had picked a mine up in the North Sea. The mine had exploded and George suffered serious injury, but survived against the odds. Another reminder of the precariousness of a life lived at sea.

Hessle Road shops, December 1964

Millers was a short distance from the fish houses and the Birds Eye and Findus factories. But for many workers, the dinner hour offered the chance to sink a swift half in the Wassand Arms or the Strickland Arms – 'Stricky'. As Margaret Green remembers, it was a common sight to see the women rushing through the factory and across the street in their overalls and wellies.

'We'd run in like 'ell, get half a lager, packet of crisps and back to work. It was supposed to be the best pint in the Stricky, 'cos the cellars was right underneath and the blokes use to say the pints of mild were spot on.'

Patricia Rudd worked behind the bar with longstanding landlord, Alfie.

'Fishermen used to come in, but they was alright. They would come home every three weeks or so with all this money, go into Strickland Arms or Rayners or Saint Andrews Club and spend their money. They used to treat you and buy you drinks and that. Some of the landlords, when the blokes were going back to sea they didn't have any money left, they would give them a bottle to take or some beer to take, tell 'em, "Pay for it next time you come home." I worked in the day for my keep and the money I got in the pub in the evening was mine.'

'Stricky' was also Marion Carlson's lunchtime local.

'We used to go in there for our hour and drink five halves of lager. There wasn't only me, all of us, it was a busy pub – all the pubs was thriving on Hessle Road. You'd prop yourself up on the line after dinner and if you felt rough, you'd put a piece of fish under the belt so it'd break and you'd get half an hour's rest while they come down and fixed it. When I was at Birds Eye, I used to do the same with carrots. You used to find the biggest bleedin' carrots – which you did – and we used to break that machine.'

On one occasion it was left to Marion's husband, Bob, to find her and bring her back to work.

'D'you know what she did one day? I went across the factory to where she worked. I said, "Where's Marion?" They said she'd gone t'toilet. I thought, toilet, it's ten past … so I goes in Stricky and says, "Is Marion in?" They said no, she'd gone back to work. She'd only gone hiding under the seats so's I couldn't see 'er.'

For most of the Hessle Road families there was a reliance on local shops, many of which have long since disappeared. Even those that remain have changed significantly. Lillian Tindle's memories of Boyes cast a light on a long since disappeared method of payment.

'In the centre up at the top there was a woman sat in a glass kiosk hanging from the ceiling with wires coming down and brown boxes screwed on the end. When you paid for your stuff the assistant put the money in the box, pulled the chain and up it went. She handled the money and then your change came back.

'Just past the Boulevard there was a shop called Leetons and they sold everything you could need for cleaning and there were two petrol pumps outside on the pavement.

'There was a brilliant cinema on Hessle Road called the Langham. It was a dream. Big foyer and lift. Bobby Johnson was the page boy that took people up in the lift to get to the cinema upstairs. The foyer was beautiful with all the film stars round. The first time I went I remember the man came out of the ground with his organ at the front, Mr Macdonald. We used to go to Langham if there was a picture on and you couldn't get in because you were kids, so you'd ask "Will you take me in, Missis?" Someone would always take you in.'

The relationship between children and their community was one based on trust. Living in Albermarle Street, off the Boulevard and close to the former Hull FC rugby ground, Patricia Rudd and her elder sister could look out of their window and see the pitch. On match day Saturdays their mother would find her garden and back yard full of bicycles. Patricia remembers the sisters' entrepreneurial spirit.

'We'd say, "Tuppence to look after your bike while you're in rugby." And they'd say "Oh, put it in then," and lift the bike over the fence, 'cos we didn't have a gate. We'd keep 'em tidy and when they come back they'd give us the money or they'd give us it before they went. We just stayed there until the rugby had finished. We did it from like eight, nine year old. We've always worked.'

The Rudd children weren't the only ones making a living from passing customers. After winning a bronze medal with his national team at the 1948 London Olympics, Danish International footballer Viggo Jensen signed for Hull City FC, scoring in his first appearance in October, 1948. John Talbot remembers, for the first two years at the club, Jensen remained an amateur.

'I was a little lad … I remember that Viggo Jensen, to earn a few extra bob he had a hot-dog cart on Hessle Road, Havelock Street I think it was. So we used to buy our hot-dogs from him.'

## Percy and Ethel Saul, shopkeepers of Hessle Road

*Percy and Ethel Saul's youngest daughter, Kathleen May was born in 1922. As Kathleen Scotney she committed her memories of her parents' lives to paper. Sadly, Kathleen died in 2012 and I am grateful to her daughter Rosanne Wilding for allowing us to use her mother's reminiscences in the following section.*

In many ways, the story of Percy Saul exemplifies a modern notion of what makes a community business. From 1919 until 1937, the family shop was a fixture at 624 Hessle Road. Percy Saul's charitable ethos lessened the burden of many local families.

Originally from Retford in Nottinghamshire, newlyweds Percy and Ethel Saul arrived in Hull on 8th October 1919. Percy had served on the Western Front in the First World War and from the outset was determined to make a go of his life in Hull and the shop he'd taken over from Mr and Mrs Pickersgill. He would be in the shop from six o'clock each morning – two hours before opening time – and would invariably work late. Often there would be customers in the shop at nine o'clock at night.

Percy and Ethel Saul and errand boy outside 624 Hessle Road

Percy and Ethel's two daughters were born in the Hessle Road shop and they had a young woman to look after them during opening hours. She sometimes helped with domestic tasks and would take the girls 'down the road'.

29

Percy gained a reputation for looking after the grocery lads who worked for him, keeping them on until they were 16. He'd encourage them look for something better, or find them a job himself. A few became managers at Meadow Dairies and Maypole Shops, two went on to drive a van for one of Percy's friends.

During the 1926 General Strike, Percy and Ethel gave food to families with children, especially making sure to look after the 'big girls' who took their eldest daughter to school at Selby Street West.

Every year, customers would be given a gift at Christmas. Depending on the size of the family and their needs, it might be a box of chocolates, a tin of biscuits, cakes, crackers, ham, pork pies, poultry, metz fruits – items Percy knew they would never be able to afford. The staff usually received a cash bonus. All year round, Percy would give away small items, pencils in silver or gold for the adults and balloons with an advert for the children.

In September most years Percy travelled to London for the Grocers' Exhibition, entering competitions for tea tasting and cheese tasting. In later years he entered the bacon boning and rolling competition in which contestants were marked for 'speed and perfection'. In previous years the prize had been won by another Hull grocer who was barred from entering as no one would compete against him, this grocer knew Percy and persuaded him to enter. Percy won once more for Hull.

Percy took pride in the shop providing high quality goods with good Danish butter bought from the 'butter boat' in a co-operative with four other private grocers. One of the grocers had a hand cart and his delivery boy collected. The other boys helped by collecting for their bosses too, on the same day every week.

At first, flour was sold loose, then in the mid-1930s Saul began to parcel in 3?lb and 7lb cotton bags. Later it would be pre-packed in paper bags for the shelf. Baking powder was made and packed in 4oz and 2oz packs each week and sugar was packed for 2d per pound. Tea arrived in wooden chests and would be blended by Percy to make the ideal tea for the local water. The tea would be sealed in red, blue, green or yellow packets trimmed with gold and with Percy's label and the price on the packet.

On entering the shop the customer would be met with the smell of the sides of bacon, particularly the smoked, hanging on the bacon rail. The aroma of freshly blended, roasted and ground coffee could be smelled as people passed the shop.

Percy and Ethel were popular and sociable figures in the community. Ethel saw that the staff had good shoes, gloves and scarves in the winter and plenty to eat and drink at break times. Between delivering orders in cold weather, the boys

Percy Saul 'Noted for Choicest Quality Provisions'

would be given tea or Bovril or Oxo cubes, which they liked but seldom got at home. On hot days they were given lemonade or a sweet drink made from ice foam crystals.

Percy often took the chair at the Carlton Street Wesleyan Chapel Anniversaries and Harvest Festivals. He opened the LNER Horticultural Show at the St Mary's and Peter's Parish Hall and handed out prizes. He also supplied the London Train dining cars with hams and other groceries at the Dairycoates Depot.

Percy and Ethel left the Hessle Road shop in 1937. A local woman with little to her name hugged Ethel and wept, saying, "If only you'll stay I'll give you half I've got." It was something Ethel would never forget.

But Percy could not settle without his business and in 1939 took a shop in Willerby. When the war came, a number of Hessle Roaders moved from the town, away from the docks, or were bombed out and they became customers again.

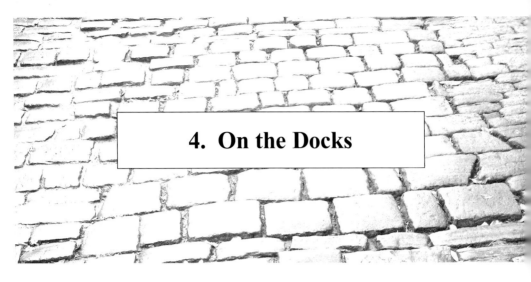

# 4. On the Docks

*'It was rough and ready, a world of its own.'*

Once fish had been landed, the industry depended on each person in a tried and tested chain doing their job. The area in and around Hull docks was populated by men and women who in some way served the food industry. Wet side or dry side, people worked hard, often outdoors in tough conditions.

In the earliest days of the industry, fishermen had landed their own catch. As fleets grew and ships and their catches became bigger, there was a need for greater manpower to unload fish quickly in readiness for the daily market. In Fleetwood and Grimsby, the men who unloaded trawlers laden with fish were called 'lumpers'. In Hull they were 'bobbers', the term derived from a 'bob haul' – a speculative catch. Employed by the Hull Fishing Vessel Owners Association (HFVOA), bobbers were split into ten-man gangs made up of a swinger, a weigher-out, four below men, a winch-man, a barrow-man and a fifth-man. In addition, each gang was allocated a board scrubber.

The gangs relied on each man's proficiency. They were highly organised, well paid and, as John Talbot remembers, worked quickly.

'You'd start at two in the morning and get it all out in five hours. Our set up was real quick, with the ropes and swinging it and all that. But we did a lot of lifting. It was three pounds ten shillings a day. So if you got five days in that's seventeen fifty – that was good pay. When I got on regular bobbing I was on a full week. But if you busted, that's if you landed more fish than the ships said, you got a gang's money shared among you. So you get extra money, a bonus see. What they call a 'buster'. So sometimes you could get twenty pound a week. Filleters might only be on twelve pound a week and you're on twenty.'

The bobbers' gangs could usually depend on the trawler's night watchman, in many

32

cases an ex-fisherman himself, for a brew of tea from the ship's galley. The watchman would board as the crew left the ship and remain there until they returned.

'Sixpence it was for a pot of tea. That was how he earned a few bob. When we'd drunk the tea, we used to leave the cup and the pot, maybe only five minutes, you'd just leave a pot there and go back to work. You couldn't leave the ships with no pots could yer? So this watchman he got the bright idea, sixpence for a pot of tea but you had to give him a shilling. You got sixpence back when you brought the cup back. Well he didn't realise that bobbers on the other ships found out what he was doing so they was taking the pots back from their ships and getting a tanner off him. He finished up with twenty or thirty bloody pots didn't he. And he was out of pocket.'

Gerry Raines was a merchant on the fish markets, working as a factory manager for Ross in Grimsby and Hull, and later with Andrew Marr & Sons in Hull. Over the years, Gerry developed a wealth of experience at buying the best fish. His 'bars of silver' could be cod or haddock that were alive three days previously.

'You would go on the market in the morning and, in the boom days, you could see over twenty-thousand boxes: by and large there was between seven and twelve thousand boxes. Your skills were in determining what you wanted to buy. It was always more difficult in Hull than anywhere else, because they landed their ships and put the fish into tubs: now you can imagine if you put ten stone of fish into a tub, you have some difficulty in finding out what the hell's in there particularly if it's small. If it's big it's not so bad – you can take two or three fish out and take a good look. You could buy what we called "large cod" from Hull or Grimsby from the deep sea fleet, at three or four stone. That's a big fish. You'd only get two of those in a kit. So the first thing was to look for the quality. You couldn't say, "I want that one, that one and that one."'

Birds Eye employee ticketing fish late 1960s/early 1970s

Until the 1950s, the wooden barrels, the 'kits', had been made by coopers working on site in lofts above Hull's Iceland Market. Arriving on the market in the morning, Gerry would tip kits over, if necessary, to get a good look at the fish inside. Crucial if he was to buy the sizes his customers demanded.

'You'd look for the eyes: if the eyes were milky, the fish had begun to go. When you gut fish, you take out the gut and the gut walls are full of bacteria, and they're the first things to deteriorate when you expose the gut to the air. The second thing you would do is, when the gut had been opened – they always gutted fish at sea – on the inside of the gut was a black membrane, and you'd just rub that with your finger and if it came off, you knew it was fresh. If you had to rub hard, it wasn't so fresh. That and the smell: you'd get your nose in and find out what it was about. Iceland was always the best fish because it didn't carry a smell. Go to Norway and you'll get Norway coast haddock: it's got an entirely different smell. Primarily because it's feeding off different grounds, whereas at Iceland the water is cold and the fish are tougher because they're in colder water – you wouldn't think they'd be colder than the Norway coast, but they are. Some of the Norway coast, the ground was soft, a lot was rocky, but some was soft: where you get soft food you always get a smell, because they feed too much.

'So you had to determine quality, secondly size. Let's say someone in Bristol wants to buy haddock fillet, they would say, "I want four stone of half-three-quarters." Half being half a pound, eight ounces; to three-quarters of a pound, twelve ounces. That takes a lot of doing, because when they catch fish, they don't say, "Can I have all the three-quarters ones this way and all the halves the other." So you catch a net full of fish which is all sizes sent by God. And at the end of the day that was the second part – get your quality right and get your size right.'

Gerry's unique position working across the Humber meant he was able to observe first-hand the distinctions between Hull and near neighbour, Grimsby. Although these were mainly white fish ports, as a merchant he needed to buy whatever his customers needed.

'Hull had quite a wide base for their businesses. We didn't only used to buy white fish, we would buy herring; twenty, thirty, forty, fifty crans of herring – a cran being twenty-eight stone. When the drifters used to go to sea, they'd take with them what were called quarter-crans, which was a metal box that would hold seven stone, so every four they put away, they knew they'd got a cran. And when customers'd ring for a price it'd be, say, forty pounds a cran. So, we were in white fish around the country: we were in herring, primarily west coast of Scotland. Predominantly, the sales of wet fish in the UK, south of Grimsby, it's cod. If you go into Yorkshire or slightly north of here, it's haddock. Now cod is shorter than haddock, so prices in the market are greater.'

Once fish had been bought, it was the barrow lad's job to take the kit to the merchant's stand on the dock. Mike Galloway had moved on from his barrow lad's job to working in the office of the fish merchant.

'It was only a little office in the stand, a box office about eight foot square: you used to look over the docks themselves, over the quayside, so you could see everything that was going on. The orders would get rung in in the morning, and I'd take 'em down. As the day went on I used to make notes out for the various customers, and the tallies – 'cos say he'd ordered ten two-stone boxes of fish, the tallies'd be pinned to side of the boxes of fish – so I used to do that, get all the tallies ready, get the notes ready and they'd be signed by the railway checker. The firm I worked for had customers all over the country and we would ring them. Our firm would have about three or four salespeople and they'd have customers spread pretty well all over the country. I can remember one, Tuckley's of Northampton. There was another one we used to send to Tooley Street in London and they used to distribute it across London, to the fish market in Billingsgate. That's the kind of set up it was.'

Mike still recalls the early 1950s minimum price for codling, the smaller cod whose size varied from around six to ten pounds in weight.

'It was thirty-two shillings and sixpence, about one pound seventy, for a ten stone kit of fish. After that it'd go across for fish meal. Usually that happened when the fish wasn't such good quality. The fish that came in early wasn't as good as the last caught. That was called 'shelf' y'know, 'shelf haddock' or 'shelf cod' and that was in really prime condition, they always paid the top prices for that. But some of the other fish, you could look at it and it'd be a bit battered really: it's been under the rest of the fish, it'd been iced in under the rest of the catch. There's nothing wrong with it, but that lesser quality fish would have gone for fishcakes and for curing.'

A surplus didn't necessarily mean fish going for fish meal. If a merchant had an excess from the day's buying, some could be stored overnight.

'You got to the box offices by these short ladders about four or five foot high, then into the office, but below them was what they call caves. So if you had fish left over you used to ice it off and put it in there, then ice it again and it'd be kept in there overnight, and next morning there'd be fish in there.

Each office – everybody had the same thing. These wooden doors used to fit in front of 'em and the fish was kept.'

One of Mike's jobs was to purchase special orders for fish not landed in Hull; the mackerel and salmon would be brought in overland and handled by a few key merchants.

'Harry Moody's was one of the firms who'd buy it. If a customer wanted an order of herrings or mackerel, salmon, or trout maybe, I'd just go and buy it. And Moody's was the place I'd go to for it, he had some overland stuff coming in. He'd have what you wanted. All the rest was landed on the dockside.

'It was hard work, but like anything once you get to know everybody it was good fun. During the winter it wasn't all that good, must've been one of the coldest place in Hull to work, 'cos you had a bit of shelter when you went in the office, but mostly you was out on the market and out on the stand really – the men who worked there, you got to know 'em and you relied on each other and there was a good craic going on.'

When Mike returned from his national service in 1959, he would have liked to have gone back on the stand with Jeff Fields, the company he'd left in 1956. It wasn't to be.

'Jeff Fields was one of the bigger fish dock companies who took over a firm called Lawson and Ashton who were a bit further along West Dock Street. They also took over a firm called Allenby's down Manchester Street. So I went to work with Bill Ashton and they were a proper old curing house, with the old kilns. When Lawson and Ashton closed down to be modernised by putting electric kilns in, me and Bill Ashton moved to Allenby's down Manchester Street and then about six months before I left to go on the commercial docks I went into Jeff Field's main place down West Dock Street.

'The curing house has gone now, but it was definitely pre-war, would have been there since the twenties at least and I think the one at Allenby's was probably a bit older. It was an older yard that one, only small and it fitted in among the houses: it backed onto houses and there was houses either side of it. If they lived down Manchester Street they could've fallen out their houses and into work, it was that close.'

As a former barrow lad, Mike Galloway has clear recollections of the atmosphere on the fish docks first thing in the morning.

'It was rough and ready, a world of its own. The sales started early morning, seven o'clock, and then the barrow lads'd follow the sales round. Say his firm bought some fish, there could be three or four barrow lads at the bigger firms, so they'd dive in and barrow the fish back to the stands to get the filleters working. Later, as the day went on, the fish was packed, and the orders came in. The barrow lads' job was to take it from the stand to the various railway wagons. Or you'd get the horse and carts – they were on the go in those days – and they'd back up alongside the railway wagons, and they'd run the kits of fish through and take it to the fish houses. I think there were about four trains a day that left with the fish. And there were general duties – getting boxes out the store above the market, or getting ice, nailing down the boxes of fish, getting ready to fill the orders.'

With a full load of fish on board and a train to catch, the barrow boys had no time to waste.

'There was a slope between the two markets and a road that ran between them over the bridge to the dry side of the dock. And if you got in the way of a barrow lad coming down that slope you'd be in trouble, 'cos he'd have to get a good bit of speed up to get up the other side with his load: sometimes he'd be really stacked out with boxes of fish.'

Mike's usual hours were from eight o'clock to five o'clock, but there was overtime when the market was at its busiest, particularly around Easter with trawlers docking until early afternoon. Ships would dock side by side with one being unloaded and another tied up, waiting. And if a barrow lad wanted to earn a little extra, there were ways and means.

'I've gone off the dock at eleven o'clock at night during the Easter week, and you'd start maybe an hour earlier. I wasn't earning a lot. I think wages for a lad at that time'd be less than two pound a week. Your overtime made things a bit better. Sometimes you could get what were called "laps".

Checking fish on quayside late 1960s/early 1970s

37

You could go around gathering laps up – when the filleters'd finished they used to leave a lap or a lug, like a little triangular piece of flesh and bone. Well if you collected a kit of that, you could go to a firm called Kilvingtons and get half a crown a kit. I think they boned it and it went for patties and things like that. Kilvingtons'd buy 'em off you, no questions asked. That's ten stone of laps, so it's a lot. Mainly cod and some haddock.'

As Eddie Rokahr remembers, the great number of companies meant there was always work for barrow lads on the market and the chance to swap jobs for an extra few shillings a week.

'If people wanted a barrow lad they'd find out what anybody else was paying and they'd put a notice on the market, "Barrow lad wanted" and pay five shillings above the odds. But in the late fifties and early sixties, five shillings was a lot.'

Being a barrow lad for Pickles on stand 191, John Talbot would travel the length of the docks several times a day.

'If my boss bought fish down other end of the market, we'd follow him to get the fish and take it to the stand for the filleters. The fish dock was over a mile long and we were right at the other end. I think there was two hundred and four stands. There was two markets; North Sea market and Iceland market. They still land the same fish. Course, if my boss bought fish a hundred stands away it didn't take long to run a few miles up in a day, back and forwards.'

Another of John's tasks was to scrub the fish boxes, never quite sure what he might find.

'Sometimes you'd send your fish – Dewsbury was one place – you send your fish and it went to market. I found out afterwards it was a market shop, selling rabbits and all that. Used to send the fish then return the boxes. But you'd always get one or two that was full of rabbit skins. They'd skin the rabbits and didn't know where to put 'em, so they'd put'em in the fish box and get rid of 'em see. And we used to tip 'em in dock and swill 'em out.'

Exposed to the elements and with no running hot water, the fish docks were never a place for anyone used to home comforts. Meeting the day's trains and filling orders on time created a sense of urgency on the dockside. On the stands, filleters worked at benches wet with running cold water, and with little shelter from bitterly cold winds off the estuary. Eddie Rokahr turned his hand to fish filleting for a short while.

'You've got to know what you're doing. I had a go and thought, I'm not standing here in running water all day with a knife in me hand. It wasn't for me, but some men thrived on it.

'Initially Birds Eye had one factory on St Andrew's Dock where everything was brought in and filleted by outside contractors. They didn't have the filleting facilities themselves. They'd farm it out to different companies who had spare filleting time, especially if the market was quiet. And they were paid on the weight return. The more meat they got off the bone the more they were paid. Every little bit that could be left on the fish would be left on. There were lots of companies doing this, the smaller firms who didn't have such a big turnover for their own business that employed casual filleters by the day or by the kit. Depending on how big it was, whether it was small stuff, big stuff – the bigger it was the quicker it was filleted so they got less per kit. Ranging from what we used to call half a crown a kit if it was the smaller stuff up to maybe three half-crowns a kit. And of course the more they turned out the more they got paid. But they weren't guaranteed the work. There were very few fully employed filleters or market men.

'I always remember one guy, unfortunately he's dead now. He was lost on the Gaul. I was working for Smarts on the market and he was filleting this fish and his knife slipped and cut his arm. He didn't go to 'ospital 'cos he was on casual. He went into the office, got a needle and cotton, stitched it up, bandaged it and went back to work. I was working in the same spot. It often used to 'appen. If they cut themselves they'd just strap it up. Those

Filleters at Brekkes circa 1970s

knives were like razors. And the number of people that cut themselves and just carried on, 'cos the majority of them worked on a casual basis.'

In John Talbot's time as a filleter he witnessed and experienced the dangers of handling razor-sharp knives in freezing conditions. Often it was so cold, the filleter wouldn't realise he'd cut himself.

'Your hands swelled up with the cold. Filleters cut their hands all the time. I had stitches in me hand. A lot of people used to get fish and fling it on a knife. Trim the fish up, flick it on the knife and a seagull'd catch it in mid-air. There was hundreds of them on the fish dock. This particular time a friend of mine, he got the fish and threw it, flicked it up off his knife and cut all the back of his hand, nearly chopped all his thumb off, cut right down. You'd sharpen your knife on a steel and once I was talking as I did it and it caught the steel and me hand went right along the blade, cut me finger right along. I've got scars all over me hands. They're worn away now.'

A filleter would usually get a pass to take a fry of fish off the docks, but for some the lure of making extra money on the side was too great.

'When I was at Pickles, they had about twelve filleters. And then when I come back after dinner one day the police are there, and about six of the filleters went off with the police. They'd been pinching fish and selling it to fish and chip shops. Course the boss realised what'd been going on and kept his books. There was a lot of fish stolen. Oh yeah a lot.'

Having spent his early working years working in fish houses, Philip Bunting passed his driving test. When he was 19, he took on a job driving.

'I used to drive in a mornin'. I'd go round collectin' pallets of wood in a Transit flat back. During the day I'd do little errands, then after dinner I'd deliver boxes of fish cakes, take 'em on to fish dock, onto the lorries to go to different towns. And then about tea time, about three or four, I'd go on all the fish dock again and get kits of what the filleters throw away. Go all along. Go to Kilvingtons, Ross Group when it was on Scarborough Street. Bring 'em back and stick 'em in the chiller. Two or three trips. This was the stuff that went into fish cakes. Just stick it in a tray, cook it, mince it an' put it in.

'In the fish docks it was always busy, always full. Sometimes there was certain drivers on the fish docks when I was driving along in me truck, and they'd come at me, two of em, side by side, and I'm thinking, "Oh no, shit!" And just before they hit, they'd part and go either side.'

Sometimes Philip would put a couple of extra boxes of fishcakes in the van to swap for fish with the filleters. Occasionally fishermen would ask a favour.

'They'd say, "Will ya take us some baccy off the dock for us, and meet us other side?" And they used to give us a couple of packets. They were only allowed so much off the bond. It wasn't great big amounts. Only fish and baccy.'

Alongside each filleter's bench would be a 'head kit' for the bones and heads of fish. One of Bob Carlson's jobs as a driver was a trip to the 'head yard' where the contents of the head kits and any unsold fish would be ground into fish meal for animal feed or fertiliser.

'I used to take fish 'eads to fish dock. When the men'd finished gutting 'em, the 'eads went down this chute for us to catch. And we used to take 'em to 'ead yard. It took half one side of dock and most of the river side; it was the biggest fish processing place in the world.'

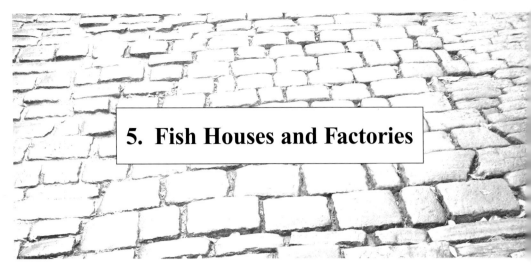

# 5. Fish Houses and Factories

*'They used to say if you were good at pattie slapping, you could put one under each arm and squeeze.'*

From the bobbers, barrow boys and filleters on the docks to the fish houses of Hessle Road and the surrounding area, the distinction is clear: the docks were a male dominated province; the fish houses certainly were not. The real work of delivering and managing factory and fish house production lines typically fell to a generation of older women, many of whom had spent their working lives in the industry. It was a brave manager or supervisor who challenged these senior production line workers. In Lilian Scott's experience younger women needed to fit in, and quickly.

'If the elder women that'd been there years and years took a dislike to one they wouldn't have 'em. They'd say to a supervisor who was over them – just say for instance it was Dougie – they'd say, "Right Dougie, I'm not avin' that little shit on this line today. I don't like her. I don't want her. Put her anywhere else but not with our gang. I don't like her work, she's not good enough." And that would be it. He might say, "Well look, she's got to learn." But they'd say, "I'm telling yer, she's 'ad over a week, we've tried, I'm not avin' 'er." And that would be it. They'd get somebody different.'

When Pearl Anderson worked at Brekkes, she was new in the trade and had taken the job in order to work a 9am to 1pm shift. It meant she could take her children, then five and seven years old, to school and catch a bus from St Georges Road to the docks.

'I was doing kippers and the guy from the other side, Jim Simpson, come in and said, "This is special order, I want skin up." You always did flesh up so the people could see what the fish was like. The supervisor come in, she said, "You don't do it like that, it's flesh up." I said, "No, it's a special order." She said, "Don't you tell me my job, I've worked here for years, it's flesh up." So I did what she'd told me. Jimmy Simpson came back, he said, "What you doing? It's a special order." I told him to go see Rosie. He brought Rosie and said, "What've you told her?" She told him I was doing it wrong. He said, "Mind your bloody business, Rosie. When I tell someone to do a job one way, I don't want you interfering." Then later in the day, my boss took me in the office – I'd only worked there a month – he said, "I want you to do line leader." I said, 'You're joking. Over this lot? No way.'"

Turning down the supervisory role made little difference to the women who Pearl had inadvertently crossed.

Brekkes Group on William Wright Dock circa early 1970s

'When I went to change me shoes, they was hidden. One time when I went to find my coat, it was missing. It's the middle of winter, I'm trying to catch the bus so's I can get to my children and me coat had been put in the toilet cistern. Can you imagine what would've happened if I'd took the job?

'At that time you couldn't be friends 'cos they looked down on yer. I'd never worked fully in a fish house, but this was my full time job. I had two children to keep, I was divorced. They never thought, "Poor bugger, she's got two kids to keep, she's got to earn a living." After that I went to work at Findus.

43

'I never went out with any of the people I worked with. They was fish house girls. I might have had to work in a fish house, but I didn't have to go out with them. They swore like troopers and they was rough women. I don't mean bad women. They drank – I didn't. I was a fisherman's daughter and in those days women never went out without their husbands. My mother never went out the door unless she was going shopping. She never went out on her own. A woman never went to the bar on her own: if she did, she wasn't a "nice person". These would: they was rough. It was the conditions they worked in. For some of 'em who'd lost their husbands in the war, they'd 'ad to be hard.'

As a young woman working in a fish house, Patricia Rudd would try not to get into conversation with the older women.

'If I was talking to somebody in the toilet and they walked in I'd back off. I used to say, "I'd better get going back 'cos they'll be shouting at me if I take too long." I'd stand my ground, but I would never confront 'em. I made sure that they knew I wasn't frightened of them. I just didn't give them an opportunity to 'ave a go. I could stick up for myself.'

That became clear when, after finishing her shift at Findus, Patricia found herself coming up against another worker on a trip to the Cholmley Street corner shop where her mother worked.

'There was a gang of women walking behind this girl I worked with. She was a couple of years younger than me. I asked her what was up and she said they were going to hit her. I said, "Stand there. Right, one at a time. I'll take the biggest first." Wham, straight in, broke this girl Diane's nose, it was pouring with blood. She was going to take her coat off, I said, "Do you want another one?" I turned round and they'd all walked away and they never touched her.

'A while later I was doing two jobs, working at Stricky Arms in the evenings. The landlord sent me a message to go and see him – he wanted to see if I could work that night. So I went in to see him at the dinner time. Anyway, this Diane had gone in and she'd been drinking. When we got back to the factory and clocked on, they caught her because she was drunk so she told them that I'd been in the pub as well, because they had sacked her. They said, "Have you been in the pub as well?" I said, "I only went to see the landlord because he wants me to work tonight – I've got two jobs, I'm saving up to get married." They said, "Well you're sacked an' all. We don't know if you've had a drink or not. You were in the pub and that's it. You know you're not allowed to go in the pub at dinner time."'

'I told him I worked there, but he wouldn't have it. This Diane was the woman who had reported me, she was the girl I'd hit. Her mother worked there too and she wouldn't let her leave the factory until I was gone. I said, "I'm not going, I'm waiting, I'll wait outside. But, she daren't come out.'

By and large the women on the production lines got on well, but as most had husbands and families, they rarely mixed socially. Patricia remembers there was always the risk that a newcomer would slow the process down and jeopardise the team's bonuses.

'You'd talk to 'em, they was company, they was all there to work. But there were bullies who would gang up on one person, someone who was weaker. And they'd say who could come to work there or who couldn't; or they thought they did. If they didn't like somebody they used to bully them so that they'd leave. It was verbal, frightening. They was very aggressive and they'd threaten, "We'll 'ave her outside." And you could hear 'em talking and the person would hear 'em taking about 'em. They tried with me, but they couldn't 'cos as soon as someone tried, Lilly said, "You leave her alone." And they did.

'I used to work on Lilly Bilocca's line you see, on her bench. They put me on her bench when I went and there was like three benches with six women on each. I stood at this end and I was cutting away. They knew I could keep up, that they wouldn't lose their bonus. You didn't just work for yourself, you worked for the other women. Because you 'ad to do so much in a day for you to get your bonus. It was on quantity and quality. They weighed all your fish and it used to be checked. They'd go through so many of the boxes and check the fish: they'd run their fingers down the length of the fillet to make sure they don't get pricked with a bone. Got a couple of bones in, that box'd be out, that's no good, you've just lost your bonus for the day.'

Lilian Scott could tell when the filleters at Birds Eye had achieved their bonus.

'That particular Friday when they got paid you could hear 'em singing. You knew when they got a good bonus, because boy did they sing every Friday. That particular month when they got their pay, the older women used to say, "They've got a good bonus this month."'

For Marion Carlson, the occasional row was a part of life on the production line. Arguments came and went and were forgotten just as quickly.

'Loads of us 'as had a set to. If you're packing and more fish was coming down 'cos they weren't doing their job further up, you'd stop the belt and go

45

mad along the line. There are so many women on the line and if they're nattering, they're letting fish go by, and the one on the end – it all goes on the end and they've to bag it and put it in collers. I'd go down the line and 'ave a go.'

Eddie Rokahr's time at Birds Eye gave rise to a personal philosophy, 'If you see two women fighting don't try and separate 'em.' Something he'd learned from experience.

'There was a kid called Mickey Gillard and these two women on one of the lines started scrapping. And Mick went in and said, "Oi come on you silly pair of buggers what's yer bother?" So they flattened 'im and then carried on fighting. Next day they were best of friends.'

Similarly, Marion Carlson was not averse to taking on supervisors. One particular run-in at Birds Eye landed her in hot water, if only temporarily.

'I told a supervisor where to get off. He had me under management so the next day I had to go. I told him what he could do with his fish. And I had to go in the next day and this bloke – one of the managers – was reading. He asked me to tell him what I'd said to Mr Porter. I told him. Well you could see he was laughing. The papers were shaking. But I got away with that – you could if you was a good worker. He didn't like me did Terry Porter. He knew my family with havin' Millers pub. And he used to go in there and me nanna used to bollock him so he tried to bollock me.'

Some women worked in the industry until retirement. As a temporary worker, for the most part Lilian Tindle didn't mix with the full time staff socially.

'I went back just for a month, because it was five pounds a week and I knew that would buy me a coat and a frock. We did an organised thing because it was Christmas. We all went upstairs and had a drink and a sandwich. Apart from that there wasn't a cat in hell's chance that you could talk. It wasn't pleasant at all really. But even then we were a step up from the women in the fish houses because working in fish house was horrendous. They had to wear big wellies and that so they always had wellie marks. At the time the fishermen used to wear red scotch scarves that were called mufflers and fishermen used to wear them around their neck. They used to bring them home for their wives and girlfriends and they used to wear turbans that went right down their back and these mufflers. They were a breed on their own; real tough lasses. You didn't tamper with fish house lasses but by 'ell they did a good job.'

'Doing the job' invariably meant working in fish houses and factories that were cold, often with running water on the floor, freezer doors opening and closing, with forklifts coming and going. The Findus company had been purchased by Swiss food giant Nestle in 1962 and the company's management staff made regular visits. Margaret Green worked at Findus on Wassand Street as the process became mechanised.

'It was called the Orenco line. Two girls slotted the fish in, it came to me and I slotted it in the machine and it was filleted. It went on from there and was processed, and it came out a pattie. All completely different, nothing done by hand, only just slotting it into machines. And I remember standing there – it was freezing and the snow was coming in on me head, I had wellies on and my feet were frozen – and I says to one of the lads, "Go and get us a bucket of hot water." I stood in it, covered it with this cloth. And this German's come round, asking, "Where's this steam come from?" I daren't tell him. Foreman after, he said, "Are you right in the head Margaret, you could've caused World War Three."'

In common with many fish house and dock workers, Pearl Anderson suffers with arthritis, which she puts down in part to the cold and wet of the factories.

'You could never get warm. I'd come home and lay in the bath for two hours just to try and warm me bones through and then I'd go to bed. You just had to try and get warm.'

As well as the cold, new workers would have to contend with the smell. Janet Wilson remembers the smell of her father's working clothes. 'He used to have to come in the back way and take his clothes off and hang 'em in the coal house and shut the door.' It's a memory that strikes a chord for Pearl Anderson.

'The flies used to whizz over yer 'ead when you was walking home. I used to come home and wash my clothes and put them in what was then the coal house. Even though they'd been washed and aired outside, you could still smell they was queenie cutter clothes. You couldn't ever get the smell out of 'em. Once you wore something for work, it was for work. I don't know if it was the smell that got up your nose, but you know what I mean … if you put them clothes on, you were sat somewhere else, you'd think – I can smell queenies on this.'

Janet's father would tour the factory at Brekkes and test the freshness of fish by eating a small piece of raw fish skin. Something Janet remembers him also doing at home. He earned a reputation as an expert and was a highly respected manager.

There were oddities among the fish brought in and a 20 stone halibut landed was regarded as a prize fish, bid for and won by Pearl's boss at Celtic Seafoods.

Alf Anderson (Right) on Brekkes factory floor circa 1970s

'There was nowhere to put it so they put it on the floor. Three days later it was still there so I went into the boss and I says, "What you doing with that halibut?" He said, "Oh, it should be sorted." I said, "Well, I come in this morning and there was a rat sat on top of it, so I don't think it's any good." He went mad, because he'd paid over the odds. He wanted to be the one who bought it. It went in the paper: this halibut was enormous. And it got thrown in the bin: it was no good. After it had had its photo took it should have gone into the filleters and they'd have cut it up.'

When Jose Verbist went for her job at Birds Eye, the smell was the first thing that hit her.

'After a while you don't notice it, it's other people. When you get on a bus they're looking at you, and sniffing, "She works at Birds Eye." You do get used to it.'

Along with the smell, Beatty Lee found the daily working conditions hard to handle and not made any easier by an officious supervisor.

'It was a very unsociable place. There was no chance of you talking, you couldn't just chatter with all the noise of these things going on, and with the Gestapo behind you it was horrible really. She was terrible the charge hand. They got her replaced by the next year and she was just a smaller sized version of the same person.

'You all went outside to the toilet for a fag regardless of the weather. It was like a square which was open and the rain came in and the toilets were at each side. You used to run out have your cig and a wee, wash your hands. It was terrible.'

Handling the fish itself came with its own hazards. Skate or 'ginny wings' could cause an allergic reaction, earning it the name 'itchy fish'. Even after washing it still oozed a slimy substance. V-boning and filleting always carried the risk of cuts. Working with bream and its sharp poisonous spines often sent any resulting wound septic. Bob Carlson remembers the advice workers were given.

'If you got poisoned in the fingers, what they advised you to do – I've done it a few times – you get a pan of water and put it on the stove and put your hand in and boil it. If it's boiling water you wouldn't be able to put your hand in, but if you bring it to the boil you could stand it. And then when your hand puffs up, you'd get the poison out.'

For some women, the casual nature of work in the fish house was an added bonus. During Pearl Anderson's 25 years at Celtic Seafoods in Liverpool Street, starting in 1982, there were frequent unannounced visits from what was then the Department for Health and Social Security.

'They'd shout, "Social security, stay where you are!" And people'd disappear to the toilets, get under the table and get theirselves hidden, 'cos they were claiming social security and working there. They come up to me once and asked for my name. I said, "Marilyn Monroe." He said, "Give me your name." I said, "Marilyn Monroe, Hollywood." He said, "I've got to have your right name." I said, "I'm legal, I don't have to give you nothing." He said, "Come on, give us your name." I said, "Pearl." He said, "Give me your name." If we found a pearl with the queenies, I used to say to my boss, "You found your pearl, me!" He didn't believe my name then, 'cos I'd messed him about that much. But we did know a girl called Marilyn Monroe. She lived at the bottom of our street, she went to our school – nothing like her, little and skinny weren't she, nowt on 'er.'

Lilian Scott worked as a V-boner at Birds Eye. She would receive the headed, filleted fish after it had been through the skinning machine and remove the V bone.

'We had to cut it out real fine. Then the fillet used to go into a tray and further along it would go to another set of girls and they used to cut off the skinny part. Now the chunky section used to go into a separate pile and the skinny part used to go into another section, squashed up into the trays for fish fingers. It was still whole fish but it was small pieces and that used to be moulded into the fish fingers and the big chunky parts used to be used for the for the fish portions. So it was all used.

'They was moulded into the blocks. Then they was taken over to a deep freeze. They was done in the small freezers then taken to a deep freeze and left there for however long, and then the blocks was turned out and then they used to go through band saws. And they was cut into sections, either into the portions to go into the batter and the crumb, or the other portions, the small portions like the cod in sauce.'

In her time at Birds Eye, Ivy Gallagher was one of the highest paid V-boners. Earning by the box, she was able to claim a significant bonus. Unlike the smaller fish houses, the larger companies provided uniforms. Workers were supplied with clogs, kept in each person's own cubby hole.

'You had to wash your own turbans but your overalls they sent them to laundry and if you ever wanted one, because sometimes you got messed up, you could have one. Then you used to wear these big white rubber pinnies as well.'

To begin with, Philip Bunting worked on the production of fishcakes. His task of making the mix started the process taking all the waste from the filleters.

'Fish bits, lugs and all the waste they threw out, that's what we used. Then eventually I got to actually mixing. You've heard of a Kenwood mixer? Imagine one about six foot tall and a big basin, two or three foot diameter.

'We put the tray of spuds in the basin, then weighed the fish on big scales and put that in. Upstairs, there's a woman doing mixes in a big bag; soya, salt, crumbs and all that in one bag. Then we put that in and got it going, mixed it. Then scooped it out of the basin. I rolled the mix to the stage where they'd put it in a big hopper that leads down to the fish caking machines.'

At Birds Eye, the fishcake making process was carried out on an industrial scale. For Jose Verbist, feeding the 'Owema machine' was the worst job of all.

'You went up these steps and there was this great big funnel with holes in it, like a sieve, you know. They brought these trolleys and there was all the odds and ends of the cod, the cod cheeks and everything. And they put them all in this big cylinder thing, with the holes in it. It all used to go in there and then they'd get it going. And there was a pipe leading from it and it used to come out "plop". There was big trays and it used to fall in to it. And it was a grey sort of a mash, you know. And that's what they make fish paste with. And they used to colour it you know and make it taste nice. That's the basis of the fish paste and other fish things, you know, fish products. Well you had your white boots on and your white oily things on and your hat on, but you also had an extra sort of a plastic thing over you, and you've got your gloves on and you used to be pushing this fish in and the men used to take the trays away and then put another one there. Beside the machine there was a great big water tank and when you came down you threw this oily thing into it. It was all covered in bits, and you felt like diving into it afterwards because you was all covered in little tiny bits of fish.'

At the age of eighteen, Jackie Gower began work pattie slapping at Rutters on West Dock Avenue. The majority of the work was undertaken by hand.

'The forewoman was a friend of me grandmother's, but me hands weren't really big enough, so when I was slapping 'em it was coming out between me fingers. I ruined 'em, so they put me on packing the fishcakes, 'cos it was easier.'

Margaret Green made patties by hand with the traditional mix of hot potato and sage laid out on a large stainless steel-topped table.

'You had a metal ring holder and you'd bring it down. You'd have a red ring on the palm of your hand, 'cos it was red hot and you was doing that all day, pattie slapping. And it went from there to being half-cooked and breaded.

'In our dinner hour, we used to go over Hessle Road and get half a dozen bread cakes and guess what we had for dinner? Pattie sandwiches. There was a little staircase you went up and a little room with a well-scrubbed wooden table and chairs, and we used to sit there and have our pattie sandwiches.

'Another day, we'd go t'fish shop and get chips and have pattie and chips. At the end of the week you could buy a box of these fishcakes for 'alf a crown and take 'em home. So I used to buy a box of a dozen, wrapped in greaseproof paper, and share 'em with me granny – she lived down Harrow Street – and me granny used to have some and me aunt Alice and me mum.'

Marion Carlson did a similar job at East Yorkshire Food Products where there were twenty women working on patties. The process was the same at each factory. Beatty Lee has a clear recollection of making patties at Summit Fishcakes.

'Somebody made the mix, the fish and potato, and the herbs. It used to come through into the factory in like a chrome bucket – it couldn't have edges on account of cleanliness. And you had a real big bench and there was girls at one end and they'd tip the bucket of red-hot mix onto a tray and you had to take it off and roll them. In between,

Worker at Summit Fishcakes 1959

51

you'd touch a cold wet cloth because it was hot work. Then we was facing them and the other tray was on a slant with breadcrumbs and they used to stand there and roll down the breadcrumbs. There was two of you each side of the tray and between you was a wire rack that you put the patties on when they was done to go into the trolleys. Then you rolled them a bit more to make sure it was all crumbed and then put them into the mould. But the stalwarts, they used to go real early to work and when you got in they was all stood checking the moulds to see if they worked quick – some of them was a bit bent and when you bashed them they wouldn't move and they was real hard. I was never early so I always got a tatty mould. So you'd have to bang it to make it come out.

'When it was dinner time and break time they used to do a special mould that they put all the best fish in for you to have a pattie for your break. They used to say, "It's break time." And we used to get our patties, but do them whatever size we liked, so you did them a bit thinner or bigger. Then they used to fry them and you would go upstairs and put it in a bread cake. And there was a table with all mugs on, and the woman who made the tea, she had a great big silver tea pot and she literally used to tip it across the cups in one motion.

'Then on a night time I used to get another pattie and go home and put it in a bread cake and go to bed 'cos I was dead tired. They used to say if you were a good at pattie slapping, you could put one under each arm and squeeze.'

Lilian Tindle worked on a similar process, bread crumbing fishcakes by hand at Stirk Brothers. As one of the smaller companies, staff turned their hand to whatever needed doing.

Lilian Tindle, Rose Dent, Eileen Lumb outside Stirk Brothers

'There were men who boiled the fish and then it was just emptied onto a stainless steel bench and the girls did it by hand, they were perfect. They'd get this mixture in their hands and there were girls lined along here that would slap them and then put crumb round them. The boss would measure and put them on the scales and there was never anything out. Everything was done by hand and then you see there was a line of you putting the crumb on and slapping: that was pattie slapping. Then they went on trays to a man who fried them. Then they were cooled and sent to the packers.

'Just before I left it became automated. The mixture went in and they came out perfect and then the crumb fell down on them, so you just needed packers. When the cakes were cooled and packed, they went out to the vans. They had four vans and they went as far as Sheffield. They did quite a good run and there used to be trains on the docks and we used to have to box them up to go on the trains, and there was a driver who just took them to the trains. His journey was just Stirk Brothers to the trains by the dock. It was hectic actually when you look at it now. We all did the same. We did packing, pattie slapping and then they went into wooden boxes with the name printed on. You used to know all the names on the boxes because their order had to be on the eleven o'clock train. They went as far as Tonypandy in Wales. I can remember them going to Cockermouth in Cumbria. As you finished you had two people on boxes right from the first cooling of the cakes. Hard physical work because you did a lot of lifting. I wasn't there long when it started to go mechanised. The man who was delivering the boxes had a box company and this particular day I was helping him unload and there was a raised platform which you had to go up steps to get to. We got talking and he said, "Come and work for me." The pay was better so I went there and was making the boxes up to when I had my first child in sixty-six. That was Needlers. They were a lovely set of people and I was very happy there.'

Pearl Anderson worked for fifteen years as a queenie-cutter. Queenies belonged to the scallop family and an experienced cutter could tell where along the coast a queenie had been caught.

'You know you get them ashtrays made from scallops, well a queenie is anything from three inches across – they was caught off Scotland – to four or five inches across – they were caught off Brid. Scarborough's were small as well. And we had to put them into ten pound bins. It didn't matter how long it took you to fill that bin, you only got paid by the bin, not by the hour. Then the bin was weighed and it had to have ten pound of meat in it and they wrote it down in a book.'

New queenie-cutters were given two weeks to learn the job, handling the long-bladed knife and building up the speed and accuracy required to earn a living. If a cutter could only fill one bin every three hours, the rate dropped to a pound an hour, whereas a good cutter could earn as much as nine pounds an hour.

'You could be anywhere from half an hour to two hours filling one bin. It was like an ice-cream container, a big one, and you earned three pounds for it. You put the shell in your hand, shell facing upwards. You had a grapefruit knife which was sharpened and you purrit across the top of the shell, took the top shell off, then you had to take all the membrane off – we called it skirts – then you was left with your piece of white meat with the roe on. Then you had to sculp it against what we called the shitbag: there used to be a bag of terrible stuff and if you caught it, it was horrendous, it always sprayed in your face. You were that used to going home with black spots on your face, you'd go on't road doing yer shopping, not realising it was all over your face. So long as it didn't get in yer eye you didn't care. You were left with a perfect round piece of meat with the roe on.

'The queenies are alive and they're trying their best not to open so you have to go in through the breathe hole at the side and break the muscle: it seems cruel I know. When you used to go in the freezer, there'd be all these green dots. All watching yer from the bags. They was all the eyes. They'd open their shell just a little bit so's they could see what was happening. And you'd bang on the bag and the dots would disappear.'

Mike Galloway worked closely with women on a curing process that, in the days prior to mechanisation, had remained the same for generations.

'Imagine the two sides of the haddock laid open with the bone still in. They were called finny haddocks, and the women used to get 'em ready for curing. They skewered them onto a tenterhook and there were these vats of dye, around four or five foot square, and the fillets'd hang into the dye. Sometimes

it'd get like a deep colour, I think it depended on the customer and what they wanted. Some would want a pale dye. It used to stain the women's hands, I know that. And the fish was hung up on these racks and then later in the day they'd get them up in the kilns. The little office we had wasn't much bigger than the one on the fish dock. It backed onto one of the kilns. And then

Tentering haddock at Birds Eye mid 1960s

54

the women used to take the fish round to the kilns – they were like a square chimney really, with rungs every so often – and then the fish would be hung inside the kiln, gradually working their way down until the kiln had filled. Then the night curer would come on as we were leaving. He'd stop through the night and in the morning the fish'd be cured and the process was reversed. The lads climbed up inside and lowered to the women down below, and they'd take the fish off the hooks, and then it'd be packed. Sometimes it'd go as it was, fresh, for various customers; other times it'd go to be frozen. It was smoked over wood chips – they used to get them from a place called West Dock Timber Company, which made a lot of boxes for the fish dock, so they'd end up with a lot of these chippings. The wood chippings were dropped into a cavity below the kiln and then the curer'd get it going, get it smoking. It was quite a nice, warm, pleasant smell. On a cold day it was alright 'cos our office backed onto it, you could feel the heat coming through. For a fish dock smell – as you can imagine it did smell a bit – it was one of the more pleasant smells. You could always smell the fish dock – if you could smell it in East Hull, you knew you were probably gonna get rain.'

After a while working on the fishcake production side, Philip Bunting found he could turn his hand to a range of other tasks. In a relatively small company like East Yorkshire Fish Products it made him an invaluable and indispensable member of staff.

'When anybody was off, like if the fryer was off, I could take over his job. I could do every job in that factory even repairing the machinery. They had a team, but if a belt broke it would come to a stop, so they sent for the people who built the machines and repair the belt. It broke down one day and I looks at it and thought, I can do that. So I fixed it. And they said in that case then – and this was middle of winter – you can go into the office and make a few belts. I was sat near a right roaring fire making these belts and it was freezing outside.

'I would start at four or five in the morning, light the boilers up, load the ovens and, depending on the day, do whatever needed doing. I'd put the kettle on and make a big pot of tea and by half-past seven everything was on and cooking. So I used to wait an hour or so and they started to come in and I had a cuppa tea ready for 'em. Then later they'd call me in to strip the machinery down while the women washed 'em all and cleaned 'em all. Then when they'd gone 'ome I put 'em all back together again. I could still be there 'til eight o'clock at night. I worked Monday to Friday and 'alf day on a Saturday.

'One day I thought I'd go 'ome early for a change. And I says to the manager, "I'm goin' home. I'll leave tonight at five, I'm goin' out." He says, "You're not, who's gonna do machinery?" I said, "Find someone else, I'm goin'." He said, "You clock off tonight at five, don't bother coming back tomorrow." So I clocked off. On the Friday I went back to get me wages and I saw the boss, Mr Hood. He says, "Where've you been all week?" I said, "Fred told me when I clocked off don't bother coming back." He said "Get yerself back 'ere Monday."'

Eddie Rokahr was a general labourer on the production lines at Birds Eye. The work varied from loading fish onto wagons in the market to bring to the factory, unloading fillets or, when fresh fish was scarce, defrosting whole fish that had been frozen at sea, ready for processing. The hours could be unpredictable.

'Anything you were needed to do you did. Many a time they would say, "Can you start at five in morning instead of six?" Then all of a sudden they'd say, "We need so and so doing. can you work on?" And this might be at seven o'clock at night. Many a time you'd do a thirteen or fourteen hour day. It was just part of the work.'

Quality control was a vital part of the production process. Birds Eye's famous claim that peas had to be from the farmer's field to frozen in two hours (this became 150 minutes in 2007) was strictly carried out. Pearl Anderson was on hand to see one delivery arrive late.

Trimming sprouts at Birds Eye circa late 1960s

'They'd been in a traffic jam and they went somewhere else; Birds Eye wouldn't have 'em. That was the rule: you could be in a queue trying to get in, but when you handed your paperwork over, if it was more than two hours; refused. Brilliant quality control. I worked on the quality control for sprouts. You'd get a big hopper – ten lasses'd get one of these each – and you'd go though 'em and if there was a maggot hole, or a bit of brown, or they was too wide open, you had to put them in different bins. And the checker'd come round and if there was too many with maggot holes, they were sent away; too many wide open from what we got given, the whole lot was refused.'

Patricia Rudd passed the courses needed to carry out her job as quality controller at Finbar. These included an instructional techniques course in 1974, a basic course in food technology at Hull Technical College, as well as chemistry and biology. Once qualified, from her portacabin in the factory Patricia would bring pieces from each line to cook and test for weight. Ultimately, if things weren't right, Patricia could stop the production line.

'I was supposed to do one every hour, so it depended on how many lines were running. I'd collect a sample off each line and then pick what they was like at the beginning so I could weigh 'em, and then also at the end when it was packed to make sure the weight was right what was goin' out to the customer. I'd check each part of the line, starting from the beginning; you've got your fish going through the band saw, that cut up into fish finger size, then it would go through this great big machine to make sure it was blast frozen, then it would go in to the batter so you 'ad that to check. You 'ad to check the batter and the breadcrumbs to make sure there was no hair in it. Women used to wear turbans, but sometimes they wouldn't wear their hair nets. If you caught somebody doing it they would be in trouble. They'd get a warning, "Get your hair net on or you're out."

'When they used to go for toilet breaks I'd take a slow walk to the toilet and anybody come out and not washed their hands, I'd 'ave a word with 'em quietly, "Look, can you come back a minute, I think you forgot to wash your 'ands." Some of them used to think you was clever, slammed the door and go out, so I used to report 'em.'

One of Jose Verbist's jobs was to examine the fish under ultra violet light. She was looking for imperfections and specifically, a little red spot.

'If you see a little red spot in a cod, usually there's a worm in it: they come through the gut in to the fish itself. So we had a little sharp sort of a knife and we had to whip the worm out and put it on the side of the board. And there used to be several of them there and I thought, I can't do it, I just can't do it. But the supervisor said to me, "Oh, it doesn't matter, it's only fish inside 'em. If you boil it, it don't matter because it's fish, just fish." And sometimes they started crawling. They were like little curly watch springs, wriggling around.'

Some of the smaller firms didn't necessarily maintain the high standards of cleanliness and hygiene of the bigger companies. Karen Rouse-Dean's brief spell working in a fish house put her off kippers for life.

'My job was hanging the kippers on to the tenterhooks. After the kippers got smoked, they used to take 'em off and dump 'em in tubs and they used to go over to the lasses and the lasses used to pair 'em and slide 'em in the bags. Then some of 'em went and made kipper patties. So you saw this nice big muscular guy with a big bowl, as big as this table, if not bigger, mixing it all. If so much fell on the floor he'd scoop it up and put it back in the bowl. If his nose was running he'd just wipe it across his arm and carrying on mixing. From there they'd make kipper patties then they'd get frozen and go in to boxes, then they'd be away. So no one knew which one was the snotty one.'

Cleaning processes were a fundamental part of the production process. At Birds Eye, the hygiene regime depended on constant checks. Eddie Rokahr witnessed one stoppage instigated by a supervisor, Ray Holder.

'He was a stickler for his job. The filleting lines were all stainless steel, everything, all the supports and everything. We was two-to-ten at Gloucester Street, when they was in there, and he went down one of the lines and he put his fingers underneath, like that, and he just shut it down. The whole of the filleting lines came to a standstill while they were washed and cleaned off because he'd found a bit of slime underneath. The factory virtually stopped until he was certain that everything had been cleaned. They had permanent hygiene crews all day and night. But he found this bit that 'ad been missed. That's how good they were.'

At the end of the working shift there was a strictly adhered to regime of cleaning routines. One of Philip Bunting's jobs, and the one he liked least, was to clean the metal trays.

'It was 'ard work scrubbing them every night. And you can imagine all fifty of 'em. You was knackered by the time you finished. They was cleaned with a big metal thing like a scourer in a massive big tank full of really hot water.'

Mechanisation altered processes that had been in place for decades and reduced the need for workers to keep production lines working. But what might have been classed as unskilled work still demanded high levels of speed and concentration. Pearl Anderson remembers the changes to the packing process.

'You'd be on the machine when the fish triangles come out the fryer on the rollers. You'd pick 'em up and put 'em in the boxes and somebody else'd fold the boxes in and somebody else'd purrit through a machine. You was in a little area, whereas in the end it was boxes of six that you had to turn them round to get them fitted in. There was a knack to 'em and if you didn't do the knack, you wouldn't get them in. It was like a jigsaw. Top, bottom, pass it on; top, bottom, pass it on. Faster than that, much faster. You'd start off in one place and if someone made a mistake you'd end up over in someone else's space.'

Patricia Rudd remembers the speed, co-ordination and dexterity with which packers handled and boxed fish fingers.

Fishfinger production at Birds Eye L to R: Ron Powell, Donald Thompson MP, Geoff Molly, Ian Wood (Wally Mole in background)

'You just couldn't pick one or two up like that off the belt and in yer box, it was that quick with all these fish fingers coming down the line. The boxes used to come down on a belt in front of you. You'd pick a box, take the fish fingers and paper and pick 'em up so you'd got five fish fingers in each 'and, then just spread 'em out – and the boxes'd be flattened out, you just flattened 'em with yer 'ands, closed the box up, then onto the next one.'

In Lilian Scott's 'thirty odd years' at Birds Eye, she witnessed many innovations and changes in process. One of which was the 'heading line'.

'That was an experience in itself that was. I was on there for about a year. You got the fish, a whole fish, and you had to take the head off, then put this fish on the belt and the machine did the rest – filleted it and skinned it and everything. There was eight of us stuck way out in the corner somewhere. It was heavy, really heavy, because some of the fish was massive. You had to stick your thumb in the eye and the rest of your hand in the gills sort of thing, and you had to sort of cut round and then you turned it over and did the other side.'

In her role as shop steward, Lilian Scott often found herself negotiating on behalf of workers who had accidents. When a woman had slipped on a metal staircase and badly cut her leg, there were questions over whether the stairs had been greasy or had she dropped the cardboard she was carrying.

'She never did get back to work. She got compensation, but she 'ad a bit of a job trying to prove whether she 'ad the proper shoes on and how come she slipped. Was it on the cardboard, was it her fault, did she drop a cardboard carton and slip on that? She said she just slipped on the stairs. But the head bloke, he took over because he said he was gonna have a job proving it and he went through everything. Eventually we got the money for her anyway, it was about thirty three thousand.'

When Marion Carlson injured her back working for Birds Eye, she also found herself in a battle for compensation. Initially the union solicitor representing her case was also working for the company.

'I was at the end of the line. And no matter who was at the end it was back breaking. Well I'd finished work at six o'clock in the morning and it happened just before six. Instead of going to somebody and telling 'em that I'd hurt me back, I went straight to hospital. So I had no proof it'd happened on the job. I knew soon as I'd lifted this thing, but it was me own fault not having reported it. But you think, "Oh, let me get going."

'I pulled all the ligaments in me back: I was in a shocking state. I never went back to work. 1996 it was. And I think I got paid off in 2001. I was on sick for that time. It's me own fault for not reporting it. They just paid me off.'

The only time Lorraine Scott remembers her mother calling the workers from the factory floor was because of an ammonia leak. 'It's got a smell like bleach, your eyes water and your throat goes dry.' After an ammonia leak or an accident, the workers would be responsible for a complete clean down of all machinery and all fish on the factory floor would be destroyed.

'We'd clean the walls, pull the machines apart. The complete lot had to be gutted and reset, cleaned. You weren't allowed to touch it. It was two days of cleaning before you could go back on to the fish.'

The importance of health and safety was emphasised to workers. A supervisor would check workers coming on shift to ensure they were correctly dressed. Lorraine remembers one lad going onto the floor in trainers who was sent from the factory floor.

'The supervisor told him to go get some suitable shoes on. And he said, "Well I forgot me shoes at 'ome." So he was told to go in the room where we keep the overalls and that and they'd 'ave a spare pair for 'im. And you 'ad to 'ave 'em on. You couldn't go in there with your sannies on or whatever you wanted.'

It meant allowing time before the shift to get dressed and clock on. In later years the clocking machine had given way to a swipe card system, but the principle remained: no one was to go onto the factory floor unless they'd washed their hands and were properly dressed.

'You had to be on the floor five minutes before your shift so if my shift wasn't 'til five o'clock I used to be there for half-past four. I used to go up to the locker room, get me clothes on and then by the time I'd come down and washed me hands – you couldn't clock on 'til I think it was ten to – so you'd clock on at ten to and then go and wait, then you'd 'ave to go your line straight away. There was no messing about, they was quite strict in that respect.'

It hadn't always been that way. When Philip Harmer first took on a management role with Birds Eye in the early nineteen-eighties, health and safety issues weren't high on the agenda. As he freely acknowledges, it was more to do with the era than any disregard for worker well-being, but something needed to change.

'In fairness health and safety has improved over the last couple of decades. For example, I would have dreaded this time of year (early December) in the eighties, because there was hardly any control on people bringing drink on to the site. Being such a social bunch you can just imagine, each group on the line would be having its own party at some stage during the week or two before Christmas shut down; which is fine except when you think about the ramifications of that. In those days, for instance, nobody actually smoked on the factory floor line but they smoked everywhere else and it wasn't thought odd that people would be taking in loads of bottles of wine and drinking them in the tea bar. But things had to change. The extremes were taken off, but the comradeship, humour and everything never altered right to the day it closed.'

Whilst filleting always carried the dangers of working with sharp knives, other accidents in the factories were rare. Marion Carlson was at East Yorkshire Food Products when her friend, Thelma had an accident as they were cleaning down.

'She took half her finger off in the mixer. She must've switched it on by mistake as she cleaned down. She was in shock: there was blood all over. They took her straight to hospital. When we see each other on Hessle Road now we still have a good laugh about it.'

The first time she worked with frozen sprouts, Ivy Gallagher got straight down to work.

'They said we had to sort sprouts out to size. Of course I went in, picked all the sprouts up and they were all stuck on my fingers and they went mad at me.

61

They said, "Get under the tap quick, don't pull them off." They can pull the end of your fingers off because they're frozen. Then they gave us gloves to do it.'

In spite of the cold, it wasn't unheard of for the occasional fry of fish to disappear off the premises. On one occasion, Marion Carlson was caught taking fish, this time for one of her supervisors.

'I never had a big bust then. Well I 'ad a big fry of fish down 'em, and I got caught. Some supervisor had asked if I'd take it out for 'im. Well I 'ad boobs out 'ere. I was frozen, nearly passed out with the cold on me heart. You think you're helping someone out. Security caught me, Harry Watson. He let me off. I was burnt with the ice. And the bloke I was takin' it out for, well, he never got no fish did he.

'They'd sack you one day and you'd go somewhere else next day. But you couldn't do that at Birds Eye. If you were caught, you were sacked. And if you were eating the products as soon as you saw a supervisor, they went down yer boobs. Or you'd put the hot fish in yer pockets.'

Jackie Gower remembers a similar experience with her friend Mary packing frozen fish at Findus.

'We had no money between us and Mary had two children, her husband was out of work. She told me to go and look for the forewoman. I said, "Alright, I'll look." And she put this frozen plaice down her pants. And then the forewoman come round and said, "You're working for an extra hour." We had a bigger order come in. Mary had the fish down her knickers for another hour before the shift finished. She took it home, but it had defrosted.'

Fish wasn't the only thing to go missing from the factory floor. Jose Verbist's friend Millie took a shine to one of the factory brooms at Birds Eye.

'We used to work together and Millie she said, "I could do with one of those brooms at home." There was a door at the side, not a main door but an escape. It came out into the yard. She wrapped it up, not the handle, just the brush, and put it outside these doors and when we went home she took it. She did, honestly. She stole the brush from Birds Eye.'

Keeping your mind on the job wasn't always easy for men and women working together. Philip Bunting met his wife when they both worked at East Coast Fish Products. There might have been separate canteens for men and women, but it did little to prevent the inevitable.

'On a Saturday, or one day in the week, we'd unload bags of spuds, four stone ones or sometimes big sacks. They'd stack 'em right high. One day I was walking through and I could hear this panting going on, and thought, what's going on round there? So I climbed up on these spuds and looked down and there was two of 'em at it. I looked down and said, "You dirty pair of buggers."'

Jose Verbist: second left; Millie: fourth left

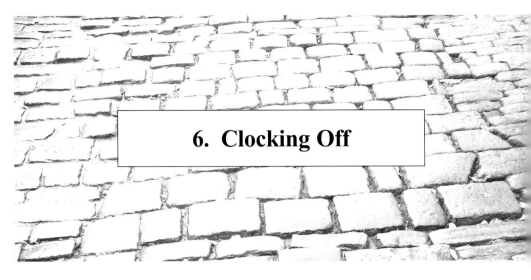

# 6. Clocking Off

**‘By the way ladies and gentlemen, we’ve got all the pattie slappers ‘ere today.’**

Whether it was a night out at Darleys or Rayners, ‘Dance Deluxe’ on Anlaby Road, or a seat in the gods at the Palace Theatre to see Al Martino sing *Spanish Eyes* or Frankie Vaughan *Give Me The Moonlight,* the workers in the docks, fish houses and factories looked for entertainment outside work hours. Local lads learned to recognise the signs in slow dances with fish house girls. Neil King remembers nights at the Mecca ballroom.

> ‘You’d get dancing with somebody and as it got warmer, slowly but surely, from certain women would come this weird sort of fishy smell which competed with whatever perfume they had on. As it got hotter and hotter it used to just rise because there was nothing they could do: it gets in the pores of your skin. They would wash it out and wash it out but that smell that came off certain people.’

It wasn’t easy for many fish house girls to get time off together with varying shift patterns and families to look after. For Ivy Gallagher, whose husband wasn’t keen on her going out, there was a simple solution.

> ‘I never told him. I used to wait until it was last minute and get ready and then off. I can remember going out to a working men’s club in Goole. We did trips every three months. The first time I went I got into trouble because me husband didn’t like me going. There was me and this other girl. She lived up in Hessle and she used to get told off from her husband as well.’

In the days of dance halls, clubs and discos, there were a string of popular venues. For Marion Carlson and her mates the evenings would invariably finish at the Strickland Arms.

'We went to Good Fellowship but we always used to end up back at Stricky. Bob used to come and pick us up – we've had a night out wi' the lasses an' that. We went to Gothenburg, which was an all-night café. You couldn't drink, but there was whisky going around. You could keep going all night.

'We never went out to the coast or anything. When Humber Bridge opened we took a coach trip and everybody went in fancy dress over the bridge. Nearly got chucked out the pub, thought they'd been invaded. It was at South Ferriby, just near the Cement Works. They wondered what was goin' on. There was A-rabs and all sorts, I was dressed as an Indian.'

In years gone by, Birds Eye, whose Hull factory had an active social club, would hold Christmas parties for the children with food and entertainments laid on. But the highlight of the year was the annual outing, usually on a Sunday in summer with families invited. Eddie Rokahr remembers a trip to Scarborough. The only workers prevented from going were those responsible for maintaining the freezers and cold stores.

Children's Christmas party with Mrs Davis, one of the organisers

'So they'd see who was goin' - it was always a Sunday – and they organised so many coaches and took us all to Scarborough for the day. You'd leave here at nine o'clock, go up to Scarborough. You'd have a mooch round, have a meal, then you'd be in the theatre for about eight o'clock. The company supplied the theatre tickets and made sure they told the artists we were all from Birds Eye in Hull. One year it was Ken Dodd and we was all sat in the audience and he says, "By the way ladies and gentlemen, we've got all the pattie slappers 'ere today." That was the only socialising we did 'cos we were on shifts. If you were on six to two you was in bed at whatever. If I was on at five in the morning I was up at four.'

In other years the Birds Eye annual outing took workers to Edinburgh for the festival. Jose Verbist had a friend, Pat Plummer, who lived on Monmouth Street. Pat's husband was their train driver for the day.

'It was Pat's husband who took us to Edinburgh. And when he used to come home he always used to pip, you know, when he was coming, when we was working in Birds Eye. He used to blow his horn. Once for I'm home and twice for put the kettle on. And I'd say, "What's three stand for then Pat?" She says, "I don't know whether he does three." I said, "Does it mean take your knickers off?" She told me not to be so cheeky.

'When we went to the festival, we started off about five in the morning. We all had to assemble at Birds Eye and then they took us there to the station. And then we all got on a train. It was a big train, a really, really old train that had like the old wooden seats on. It was ever so rickety, going all the way there. And when we came back to Hull I think it was at five in the morning. All that way we went, all in one day, y'know. But it was really nice. The train was full of people, maybe a couple of hundred, something like that. There was a lot of us. I think they paid part of it.

'And then another trip we had we went to Ostend. I don't think that they paid for that. It was sort of subsidised. We went on the ferry from Hull and we were there, I think probably a couple of days.'

Birds Eye family outing

After a night out for fish house workers, there was no respite. The shifts may have been flexible, but there were limits. Pearl Anderson's hangover cut no ice with her boss at Celtic Seafoods.

'They didn't care what time you went in as long as you did four hours. You either had to do four hours or two bins before you could leave. I once went in with an hangover when Lil Scott's first girl got married on the day before New Year's Eve, so I had to be in work on the New Year's Eve to get me holiday money. I went in and I had a head like a bucket. I used to drink Pernod and someone said, "Have a drink." And I had a drink and oh, I was bad, I've never been like that since, and I said to the bloke "I've done half a bin, let me go home." He said, "No, you don't get your holiday pay unless you've done two bins or four hours." This woman said to me, "Here's a bin and a half, go weigh 'em in, and go home and give me 'em back next year." I hardly ever went out, so they knew it was bad. So she gave me her fifteen pound of queenies and I went home and when I come back, my first bin and a half was for that girl.'

It didn't matter how serious the situation, the shift ran by the clock. Lilian Tindle worked close to home on Hessle Road. 'You came home for lunch, you had an hour. I used to walk from Rugby Street to Constable Street and mum always had it ready.'

'My boss was a horrible man. It was the sixteenth December 1958 and it was about half-past one and my sister-in-law and brother came to say my dad had died, and of course I burst into tears. I got my coat and the boss whistled and shouted, "Oi". When I looked he was pointing at the clocking off machine. You clocked on and clocked off and if you were minutes out your pay was stopped. Dad's funeral was in the morning, but I went back at lunch time because the money had been stopped in the morning. You got paid exactly what was on that clock.'

Lilian's best friend left the factory to train as a nurse and eventually, after some persuading, Lilian joined her. They remained in the profession and were lifelong friends.

After leaving Birds Eye, Eddie Rokahr became a bus conductor. On his route along Hessle Road, Eddie's run included the 'tea time back-up', an extra bus scheduled to pick up the overlap from Smith & Nephew as the factory shifts ended.

'The regular service man would fill up and go and we'd pick up who was left. But the next stop down the road was this fish processors called Eskimo Seafoods on Hessle Road and if you weren't full you'd get so many on.

We'd pulled up and 'ad room for three. Well at the time one of our crews 'ad been fined a week's wages for overloading the bus. There were a set number of people you could carry; it was eight standing. This guy got on and says, "I ain't getting off." So I told him we weren't going nowhere. He says, "What do you mean?" I says, "We're not goin' nowhere." So I just give my mate three bells – if you rung the bell three times he knew there was something wrong at the back. So he come round. He says, "What's up Ed?" I says, "This guy refuses to get off." He says, "Are we overloaded?" "I says, "Yeah, he's the ninth standing." So my mate the driver's sat on the stairs. He says, "Whilst you're still there we're going nowhere." Well this young lass got up who'd been working in the fish factory. And she had the old, what we used to call clumpers, wooden sole, steel ring on underneath and leather top. She says, "Are you getting off this bus?" The bloke says, "No." She says, "You are." And she laced 'im right in the family jewels with her clog. She says, "I'm wet through and I'm goin' 'ome, now get off." She says, "Can we go now conductor?" I says, "Course we can love." And away we went.'

The women who worked in the factories were a regular sight in the streets of the city. They carried their colour and vitality with them into the community and onto the buses. Neil King remembers travelling on buses as the fish house and factory shifts ended.

'In those days, you could smoke upstairs on a bus. In the winter a double decker bus would all be steamed up, full of condensation, full of people. Added to that nearly everybody on the bus was smoking so you had kind of thick fug and as it got warmer and warmer and these women got on, the smell of fish permeated it as well. So you had this really horrible sort of solid, fuggy mess of smelly smoke.'

As a teenager, Neil remembers the factory girls were good for an illicit Player's No.6 and a chat. Older men who ventured upstairs took their life in their hands.

'You would see blokes going up the stairs on the bus looking to see how many were on, starting getting the abuse and going back downstairs. They used to chuck stuff out the window at blokes going past as well so they would slide the little top window open and shout at people.

'There was one woman who used to work in a fish house, I don't know what she did but she was always on a bus on a Sunday night going down Anlaby Road. She was a real nice woman, youngish. She worked in one of the factories and she always had this routine on a Sunday night. We used to go to this place in Hull, which is now Hull Truck, but it was a live music place.

We would come out, get on the bus and she would always be on there and she'd have her fags and a bottle of cider, which she would share with anybody, and she'd play what we would then call a Jews harp, jaws harp they call it now. You know one of those old things you stick in your mouth and it would twang. She used to sit on the bus every Sunday night singing songs and playing this thing and people'd just sing along.'

# 7. Doing Business

*'In Hull it was home from home, because it was fish. It felt like going back, being more hands on, and I loved it.'*

From traditional, individually owned companies like Harry Moody's, Braham's and Hill Brothers with only a stand on the docks and a barrow lad and filleters on the books, to the larger fish houses such as Jeff Field, Lawson and Ashton, Allenby's on Manchester Street and Stirk Brothers on Subway Street and Flinton Street, to the multi-national corporations of Ross Group, Findus and Birds Eye, the fish processing industry was by far the city's major land-based employer.

Inevitably with shifts in customer taste, the rise and influence of supermarkets, and the demise of the fishing industry, the processing industry changed. When Patricia Rudd returned after some time away, the environment was quite different.

'The quality was still the same but the customers expected more. Asda and Tesco, Marks and Spencer's, they used to come round and look at the factory themselves, and if it wasn't spotless, we wouldn't get the contract. Every woman there had to be covered, every man's hair had to be covered. It got stricter because they were expecting more, the quality you know. The factories got bigger and so did the machines.

'It was the same staffing, maybe more in some places. They went into making different things, like they went into making beef burgers, and then they used to go into grill steaks and then meat, you see. Then they used to do pies. They had all the ranges you see. They didn't just stick with fish because then, after these trawlers had gone over so many years, the fish and trawler industry just stopped. So the factories expanded into different things.'

Lilian Scott remembers the exacting standards imposed by the supermarkets. If a product was in any way imperfect, it could be sold in the Birds Eye factory shop as 'seconds' or sold on to discount supermarkets.

Birds Eye factory shop

'They was still alright, but if it wasn't up to the Birds Eye quality it would go to seconds. The cod in sauce was the one that was spot on. And Sainsbury's, there used to be an order with Sainsbury's. They lost their order because they wasn't up to the quality that Sainsbury's wanted. They wanted a lot of good quality for a cheap price you see and it wasn't good enough.'

As early as 1949, John Carl Ross has expressed concerns about over-fishing in the northern waters, writing that, 'many seem to assume that Providence will provide the fish ad infinitum.' He believed the fishing business would result in the survival of the fittest, declaring '… that is what we intend to be.' It was this concern for the future of the industry, and the wish to reduce the losses incurred when trawlers landed catches in an already crowded market, leaving the company, the ship and its crew in debt, that drove Ross to diversify and invest.

As a boy, Gerry Raines had watched trawlers come and go from Grimsby docks on Saturday and Sunday mornings. He would sneak onto the market to watch the merchants buying and selling. In 1952, on leaving school at the age of 15, he began his career with Ross Group in Grimsby. After his National Service he returned to the company and would become factory manager of plants in Grimsby, Lowestoft, then in 1968, Hull. His success there saw him return south of the Humber with overall responsibility for production at all five Ross factories. As well as fish, there was vegetable production, ice cream, and meat products. Eventually the pressure took its toll.

Gerry Raines at Ross Group 1966

'Two years later, I was taken away from it because I'd had too much stress. But went back eventually and set up a new chilled division. This was around 1979.

And at that stage there were these little packs with fresh fish inside that had extended shelf life via gas flushing, and we were the first to put it into supermarkets. Little shallow trays overwrapped and gas flushed, which had something like five, six or seven days shelf life, which was the beginning of the chilled era in fish.

'In those days we were talking about the likes of Fine-Fare and Keymarkets, and those people as opposed to the Marks & Spencer's and Sainsbury's of this world, who were a long time coming into the chilled business.'

After a serious disagreement with the Ross Group chairman, John Foulkes, Gerry received a phone call from Arthur Amos, fish processing manager for the Hull company, Andrew Marr & Sons. 'Arthur said, "What've you been doing, sleeping with the chairman's wife?"'

Word had reached Arthur Amos on the industry grapevine that Gerry was looking to move on. He went to work for Marr & Sons.

'It was much the same as I had done in my early years. I went on the fish market, bought produce as I'd always done. Wherever I'd been I was always one of the buyers of fresh fish. I started over there in July 1984 working for this chap Arthur Amos, who wanted to retire, that was hastened on by Andrew Marr himself, and four of us bought the company in a management buy-out. So we changed the name to Marr Frozen Foods. We were in Gillett Street, off Goulton Street. That used to be the area to live if you were a skipper or a mate or a bosun or whatever.

'Going back to Marr was easier, a lot less stressful. In Hull it was home from home, because it was fish. It felt like going back, being more hands on, and I loved it.'

Gerry's experience of working the fish markets on both sides of the Humber gave him an insight to the differences between the two.

'Grimsby had what we call a mixed fleet; they always had near water, North Sea; middle water, which is Faroe, West Lean; then we had deep waters, so we had a real mixed fleet. In Hull, they were ninety-nine per-cent deep water, Iceland, Greenland, you name it. Hull had the volume. Back in the late nineteen-sixties, early nineteen-seventies, I've gone onto Hull market at six o'clock in the morning and there's been twenty thousand boxes of wet fish to be sold.'

With Marr Frozen Foods, Gerry would look after companies outside of Hull. These were seven well-established wholesale fish merchants who provided fresh fish for shops, stores and restaurants around the country.

'We had Bristol for the south-west, Middlesbrough for the north-east, Mansfield for the east-midlands and so on. And we'd send fish there. It lifted the distribution problems – you couldn't really do that centrally. Distribution was a major factor in the way the whole thing's gone anyway. I looked after the depots and my element of the company after the buyout was looking after the wholesale fish side.

'Gradually as the industry changed, supplies became more difficult. The decline in the fleet was greater in Hull than it was in Grimsby, because Grimsby had a more modern fleet. And they were all deep water in Hull, which were older and bigger vessels. The fish business changed, supplies were depleted and I gradually closed the companies down.

Gerry pinpoints the unique nature of the business. In a large national and multinational company, he was responsible for profitability.

'If you take the frozen food producers of today, they have buyers who buy the produce from wherever, they have their own sales team, they have their own marketing team, but even then they're not responsible for net profits. Whereas in the business in the old days, and certainly in Ross in my experience, we were totally responsible for the net profit. So you didn't only have your buying ability to get right, and your ability to make sure it was done right, the right fish put into the right boxes, but you had the responsibility to make sure the customer got what he wanted, to make sure the sales guy was off his backside and round the country to make sure it all happened. All part of the management role.

Ross Group factory floor circa 1964

'In the old days, Ross used to train managers and they would go all over the world, because they'd had commercial training. Every Friday afternoon I wanted the *Net Profit Weekly* on my desk at two o'clock. It had to be there because you wanted to see the sales guy before he slipped off for the weekend, and say, "Well we're not doing *that* next week."'

As one of the UK's best known producers of frozen food, Birds Eye produced some of the country's leading brands of fish products and frozen vegetables. The company regarded the Hull and Grimsby factories as a single entity. As manufacturing manager of the fish operations, as well as Chief Engineer, Philip Harmer was responsible for Hull's No.1 Building.

'I was really nervous about that job. I was comfortable within engineering, but then all of a sudden I was responsible for seven hundred people in that unit. But the whole atmosphere, the way that the ladies worked amongst themselves … If there was somebody who wasn't working at the same rate as the majority, they either got them up to that speed or they'd want them off the line. It was great actually when I think about it. It's a pity it's been lost. We had supervisors and charge hands and all the rest of it but those teams that were packing, it was very labour intensive.

'It was hard work as well. We had ladies loading blocks of frozen fish on to the lines at the speed of the line; I mean we're talking three tons an hour, which is a lot, incredible really. Occasionally we'd go on to the line to see if we could do it, to get a feel for what it was like, but there was no way could we keep up, physically or from a dexterity point of view.'

One of Eddie Rokahr's tasks was to handle the fish in and out of the defrosting kilns. Buying fish that had been frozen at sea (FAS) was one way of ensuring the best price at market and a guaranteed supply.

'These three-month-trip freezers, which froze the fish whole at sea, they'd go and buy a load and put it into cold storage so that when the markets was low they could just drag it out. It used to come in ten stone blocks, just a big block of frozen whole fish. So all we had to do was get it in the kilns to defrost it. We used to have a metal stand on the floor, it was like a domed shape. We'd pick these lumps up, drop it on the dome and separate the fish. Then it had to be loaded on to trays and in to defrosting ovens. That could be 'ard work.'

Working for Birds Eye was regarded by most a job for life. The company was recognised as a good employer that looked after its staff and offered 'good perks', a particularly attractive prospect in an industry traditionally populated by casual workers receiving few, if any, benefits. As a Unilever company, the factory shop offered a range of reduced cost products. Lilian Scott remembers staff would receive either a turkey or a bottle of sherry with a voucher at Christmas.

'And on your birthday they'd give you a voucher. After fifteen years I got a gold bracelet and a meal, you always got a meal. Then after twenty five years I got something else. You did get looked after.'

As a former employee, Jose Verbist continued to receive an annual Christmas parcel from Birds Eye.

'We never got a pension but every Christmas we always got a parcel. There was tins of stuff, you know, like tea and coffee and biscuits, a big parcel. Sometimes my son used to come up and bring it home for me.'

Marion Carlson worked for a number of companies, but none compared to Birds Eye for flexibility of shift work.

'Years before, when I worked at Eskimos, you could walk out one hour and get another job. It was better to work for one of the bigger companies, although Birds Eye was more strict. They tret you like slaves. There were too many managers. You couldn't get away with much, not that we didn't try. But Birds Eye paid better. I started on five to ten, then I did seven till twelve, or ten till two, and then I went on all nights. That was ten till six in the morning. That's when we did vegetables

Marion Carlson at Birds Eye

in one season and then we was brought across to Factory One to do fish after veg season was finished.'

The management culture at Birds Eye was primarily set by its parent firm, Unilever, a world class, Blue Chip Company. This meant that individuals were actively encouraged to experience more than one area of the production process. For Philip Harmer to become a Chief Engineer, he had to have been a Manufacturing Production Manager for at least three years to learn all-round skills including production management, marketing and finance. He was one of the few 'home-grown' senior managers, with most originating from the Unilever Management Trainee Scheme. Technicians and supervisors could be employed from a wide area, but the main factory workforce lived within walking distance of the Hessle Road site.

'I didn't realise at the time how much it was giving me. You only see the area that you are in. But then I realised how much benefit I got from the Unilever and

Birds Eye model. So it doesn't worry me if I go in somewhere in a manufacturing role or whatever. From a business point of view it was a natural progression.

'I think it is unique to companies like Birds Eye. Lots of people benefited from that. Because it was never an autocratic business of lines of management. You talk about the production teams; they were self-managing. As long as it was clear to them what was required then they always found the best way of doing it.'

The Birds Eye ethos spread throughout the organisation. However, the changing nature of the company, its products and the numbers of workers required for the production process meant that Birds Eye employed more agency staff. There was a need for a more flexible workforce. Phil Harmer explains how this worked in practice.

'We produced a product called "Simply Fish" which went down really well and it was developed locally as well which was great. It was a natural piece of fish fillet, not sawn, that had to be hand loaded in to plastic bags and then the plastic bags went in to a carton. Because it was such a premium product – it still is – that if there were six in a big carton, we wanted, rather than trying to fold the box down and try and fit it back in your freezer, it had a plastic bag inside it so that you could discard the carton and then fold the bag down. That took a lot of labour, so in the middle of a week you might suddenly require an extra twenty ladies across a couple of shifts, so there's forty people just straight away that you need to flex in and out. So there was a lot more agency.

'They tend to be slower, but we mixed them with people who were on the line. It went pretty well, better than you might expect. The key to it was that the pay for the agency people was exactly the same as our own people. It was a good pay system at Birds Eye, anybody would say that. From a union point of view, and it was GMB there, we had an agreement that the number wouldn't be above I think it was fifty, so we'd discuss if it ever had to go above what was the agreed number.

'But a lot of the agency staff were ex-Birds Eye people who, for instance, had left for family reasons and then it suited them to come back in. Or even people who'd maybe been widowed and things like that. There was always encouragement for other people within the family to work there. Birds Eye positively encouraged family members to work for the same company.'

Pearl Anderson remembers the arrival of 'Simply Fish' and the changes in working patterns. She wasn't convinced.

'Skinny things, fillets, they didn't look right. Then it was just the loin, so's it was just the nice pieces of fish. There used to be thirteen people on the packing line. And we ended up with four – two girls up there and me and one down here. The machine used to weigh the fish, drop it in a bag, the bag come round dropped on the line. When it dropped onto the line, it dropped into the box, then it used to be stuck down. They saved our wages by buying this machinery.'

Lorraine Scott remembers the arrival of agency workers.

'At first it was alright, but they was putting them on the line and we 'ad to train 'em up. There was a lot of issues about that. Some of them, y'know, like the foreigners that used to go to the agencies, they used to shove 'em in and they'd be there a couple of days. But they'd to say to us, "Can you just train 'em on that." And I used to say, "Well I'm not training 'em I'm not getting paid. Why should I train them?" It wasn't the same people twice on the trot. There'd always be new ones. Some of 'em picked it up alright but some of 'em were useless.'

As a former shop steward at the Birds Eye factory, Lilian Scott's perspective on staff and management relations focused on pay and conditions. She acknowledges there was tension between staff and management.

'You 'ad yer ups and downs. It was mainly disputes over pay and things like that. There wasn't so much later on; there didn't seem to be that unity. People were more worried about losing their jobs.'

Changes to methods of working often caused issues amongst staff used to carrying out tasks in a particular way. The company prescribed a standard method of how products would fit onto pallets and packs would into a case.

'You 'ad to stack yer pallets a certain way, but people'd been doing 'em the way they did them for years. Fetching them changes in was 'ard. And the way they was saying you 'ad to do 'em. I mean I stacked pallets the way I did 'em, I'd been doing 'em that way for years. I'd got into a routine and it was the easiest way.

'There was more lines coming in as well. They was takin' staff from one part and putting 'em on another part. I'd said, "You can't do that because you need yer staff." And this was what a lot of the disputes was over because they was cutting the staff down and they was saying, "Well you can do it, if you can stack yer pallets like this." But you couldn't do it the way they was saying and there was no way you could do it and 'ave a woman short. You'd be doing stacking for five hours and some of 'em would be doing it for eight hours.'

For years the teams had worked out their own breaks, but when the company introduced structured break-times, production line staff felt they were being short changed.

'They'd cut the breaks over time. Down to one break in five hours, whereas before we sort of worked our own breaks so there was at least two to three breaks in five hours. We'd worked it amongst ourselves and with the group. You'd work that bit 'arder and you'd get round, but then when they come and said, "Well you do it this way and you do it that way and we need that extra woman and you 'ave one break."

In later years, despite a healthy membership of the GMB Union, Lilian sensed the decline in union strength.

'It sort of dwindled off. And I noticed they didn't seem as strong. Then I couldn't get off for me meetings as much because I couldn't get cover, so I used to say, "Well, I'm sorry I couldn't come to the meeting, but I'm not leavin' the girls on their own."'

A 1978 edition of the newsletter produced for the Birds Eye factory at Hull gives an insight to the relationship between staff and management. Under the heading: *Industrial Action At Hull*, the factory's general manager, Mr B. J. Hasberry, wrote:

*All of us at the Hull Factory have been concerned about the future of the factory in recent months. We all realise the problems outside our control, such as fish supplies, can create for the factory.*

*Against this background, it is very disturbing when we have to face self-inflicted wounds like strike action which can only damage the factory now and for the future.*

*In a community of 1500 people it is inevitable that we have differences of opinion between us from time to time. However, we do have Grievance Procedures with all Trade Unions on site, to allow these problems to be resolved.*

*Let's make sure that these procedures are followed in future and that we avoid a hasty strike that harms no one but ourselves.*

# A LITTLE BIRD

JUNE 1978      EDITION Nº 9

## INDUSTRIAL ACTION AT HULL

"All of us at the Hull Factory have been concerned about the future of the factory in recent months. We all realise the problems that factors outside our control, such as fish supplies, can create for the factory.

Against this background, it is very disturbing when we have to face self-inflicted wounds like strike action which can only damage the factory now and for the future.

In a community of 1500 people it is inevitable that we have differences of opinion between us from time to time. However, we do have Grievance Procedures with all Trade Unions on site, to allow these problems to be satisfactorily resolved.

Let's make sure that these procedures are followed in future and that we avoid hasty strike action that harms no one but ourselves".

B.J. Hasberry.
Factory General Manager.

## SOCIAL CLUB NEWS

**Annual General Meeting.** The A.G.M was held on 24th May at the Cherokee Club. The past year had been very successful and a record 17 events had been organised. Officials of the committee were re-elected along with three new members. The meeting was followed by a very successful disco and it is now hoped to organise further events at the Cherokee.

**June Disco.** Because it clashed with the World Cup Final this function has been re-arranged for Sunday 18th June, although we hear the ladies have already had enough football. The venue is Juliets price 75p including basket meal. The Miss Birds Eye contest will be held on this evening. Prizes, £10, £5 and £2.

**York Races** The trip to York Races is now on for Saturday 15th July. Buses will leave Hull at 10 am and people can do what they wish in York. It is expected that one coach will leave York at 11pm and one at 1am the following morning. Watch the notice board for further details.

**London Weekend.** We are still going ahead with a weekend in London and trying to get the most competitive offer. Already a number of people have shown interest, anyone else please give names to S. Melia, Fish Products or I. Bielby, Veg. Repack.

**Holidays '79.** A meeting was held in the main canteen on Sunday 4th June to discuss holiday arrangements for next year following the success of the Benidorm trip. It is intended to offer the following holidays to members and guests.
1. Torremolinos – Last week in April 1979 (7 days)
2. Benidorm – End of April 1979 (11 days)
3. Arenal (Majorca) – 23rd August 1979 (14 days)

Only fifty places will be accepted for any of these holidays so interested people should contact any of the following Committee Members immediately. D. Inglis, R. Artley, S. Melia, R. Bielby.

**Sports Day.** Sports Day will be held at Bethune School on Saturday 24th June. Transport is to be provided from the City Centre, Bransholme and Orchard Park. All arrangements have now been made and all that is required for a successful day is a good turnout, so please come along and give your support. Programmes are available around the factory.

**Future Events.** Two events planned for the future which you should all put in your diaries. Saturday 26th August, Dance at Jacksons Ballroom and Saturday 21st October, Darts and Dominoes Disco at Hessle Town Hall.

## WHAT ARE YOU WONDERING?

– Do the Sports and Social Club supply false teeth?
– Are the people who inform local retailers about cheap shop sales jeopardizing future offers?
– Who finally hit the jackpot after ten years of rainy holidays?
– Are we to employ a a lollipop man to help you across the road?
– Who missed his wife's birthday yet again?
– Was the competition at the fishing club dance won by a muscle or mussel man?

## ON THE MOVE

**Production Supervisors.** Two production supervisors are currently on the move. **Ted Welham** left us last month after 17 years service. Ted who supervised on Veg. Repack had spent a great deal of time as Night Hygiene Supervisor. **Percy Littlewood** is to leave us at the end of this month after 16 years service, mostly spent on Fish Processing. Percy and Ted were in at the start and over the years have made a large contribution to the success of the factory.

**Tony Bowsley.** Engineering Planning Supervisor - Tony is to leave at the end of the month to join the Arabian International Construction Company, as Works Engineer. Tony is to work on the construction of the new town of Jedda in Saudi Arabia. Tony was well known for his work as Secretary of ASTMS the management and supervisory Trade Union.

**Beryl Whipp.** Beryl after a fairly short stay as Sister-in-Charge has resigned and is to leave us shortly.

**Footballers** Another blow to the Hull factory's flagging footballing fortunes is the departure of two long serving employees from the Fish Processing Department. **Gordon Sanderson** left recently after 9 years service. Sandy has for many years been a stalwart of the Birds Eye local soccer team. **Roy Bunce** is to leave this week after 9 years. One of Hulls longest serving top amateur players Roy is well known to company footballers as the skipper of Hull Chairman's Cup team for many years. Roy will be remembered by the Chairman and directors for his reluctance to make speeches at after match meals.

I understand Sandy and Roy are to work for British Rail.

On behalf of all friends and colleagues we wish all the above people future success.

## CANTEEN OFFER

Available this week at the Factory Shop are limited quantities of John Wests tinned fish and meats. Also on offer are various jams, canned fruit, biscuits and other assorted items.

Birds Eye newsletter June 1978

In some companies, trades unions found gaining a foothold more difficult. Philip Bunting was instrumental in running a branch of the Transport and General Workers Union at East Yorkshire Fish Products for a short time in the early 1970s.

'We did get some things done. We got the toilets improved for a kick-off: the wash basins and all that. This kid who was running it, he left. He asked did I want to take it over? I did and it was alright for a while, but the managers didn't like it. One day someone said I was wanted upstairs in the office. I thought, now what've I done? And I goes up and Mr Rudd, the gaffer, he says, "You know this union, Phil. How 'bout a few more quid a week. Would you scrap it?" I said, "Depends 'ow much." He said, "Will an extra fiver a week do?" A fiver then was a lot. I said, "Yeah, fair enough." And the union was gone. Nobody bothered. The main problem was the peculiar hours I was working. I had keys for the factory. I was first in and last out.'

For Gerry Raines, dealing with trades union issues was a time-consuming and particularly unrewarding part of his job.

'I had to spend fifty to sixty per-cent of my time – especially in the latter years – with trades unions, trying to solve problems. On the Grimsby site we had AEU, G&M, the office one – I can't remember, but we had seven trade unions, and you just spent your time talking and talking. I wouldn't deal with unions conning the workforce. So I couldn't sit in front of trade union people and say things like some others did and I used to cringe. We dealt with unions a lot of time and it wasn't particularly enjoyable.

'In Grimsby we had eighteen hundred people at our lowest ebb; we had three-thousand when peas were on. In Hull I had six hundred and twenty-four. It was easy. What I found was that, at the end of the day, your ability to recognise people's ability, people's understanding was very important, because in Hull I used to take my weekly figures into the meeting room. We used to have a lecture theatre in Hull, and I would take a group from the factory and tell them how we'd got on, and show them how we'd done £10,000 this week, how insignificant that was in the scheme of things. You could do that because you had smaller groups.'

There is no doubt that the region's expertise in food processing management and production was among the most efficient in the world. This was confirmed when Birds Eye received one of the world's highest awards for manufacturing. Philip Harmer stresses that The Total Productive Maintenance Award (TPM) from the Institute of Plant Maintenance in Japan is not won lightly. He flew to Tokyo to receive the award on behalf of the Hull and Grimsby factories.

'It's measured on how effective the teams are and how self-motivated they are. We talk about the comradeship and everything, but these ladies knew how to work in a world class environment without even thinking about it and would just fit in and get on with it. So lots of people grabbed them to work for them.'

With Unilever operating factories throughout the world, there was a need to establish a standard which compared workers in a factory in Hull to workers in Indonesia.

'They went into the TPM structure where the consultants came from Japan, and I mean really senior guys: one guy that came to measure us used to be the works director for Honda in Japan. They would come round to the sites and monitor and if you got to a certain standard then you'd get a certain level of award and both Hull and Grimsby got the Excellence Award for Total Production Maintenance.'

The skill, efficiency and professionalism of the Birds Eye factory workers aside, one particular memory sums up Philip Harmer's experience.

'People tended to have their name and the area where they worked on their coats. Let's say the lines would be typically AB1, which is Aerated Batter – people from Birds Eye would know these absolutely – CIS, Cod in Sauce, that kind of thing. And there was an area where we prepared the fish cakes and it was called the Pattie House, so they'd have Pattie House on their coat. Anyway this lady started and I think her husband had a particularly good job, they lived in a really nice house in West Ella I think it was, and when her husband died she came to work for the social side of things for Birds Eye. Really nice lady and she was in the tea bar talking to people and she said to me, "I love it here, the people are so nice. I was just talking to somebody this lunch time, she was so helpful." I asked who it was. "Pattie Hoase she was called." And it was the Pattie House that was written on her coat. To me that summed it up with Birds Eye, the fact she felt so proud of it. She'd have been calling this woman Pattie and that'd have gone on 'til she left and nobody would have corrected her. They'd have been nudging each other.'

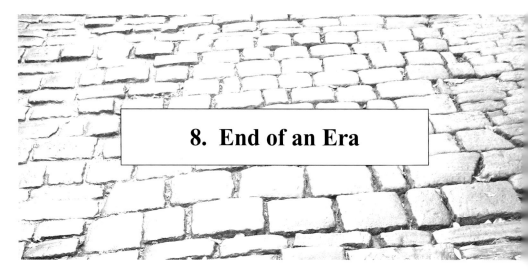

# 8.  End of an Era

*'If I drive down Hessle Road and I come to Daltry Street fly-over, I can always smell it just in that one area. I can smell it plain as day.'*

As the industry scaled down, work became scarce. Like many workers, despite a lifetime of experience, Pearl Anderson found it difficult to find employment. There were those willing to take advantage of the situation.

'I worked at a place called Pashminas – they'd got on the tailcoats of Celtic Seafoods. I'd been there six months, paying tax and everything and I found out they wasn't paying it in. They just absconded one night. One morning the lasses went to work and they'd gone. I was queenie cutting there as well, about six months. I used to go to Celtics and if I was waiting too long for work to come in, I'd go to Pashminas and work a few hours there and go back to Celtics and see if the work'd come in.

'I went eighteen months without work. I don't know what happened, they used to say that the sea was getting over-farmed. There was nowt else doing, and so I went with an agency and went to work at Birds Eye.'

The final few months for Bird Eye left workers with uncertainty. Pearl was one of those ringing in each day to see if there would be work and finding the only voice at the end of the phone was an answering machine.

'It'd say, "There'll be no work tomorrow, but ring up tomorrow." It depended on the weather in Scotland, whether the boats could get out and ger' enough to bring down here. If they couldn't they'd keep it in Scotland at West Coast Fisheries. But if they had a load, they'd come down to us. So we never knew if we was gonna have work, but we had to ring in every day.

'They were investing right up until the end. They had another line put in. They had to get it working perfectly and numbered so it could be moved. The person who was in charge of the line went with it, so he could set it up in another place, train up the girls who'd work it. Loads went to Russia, Germany. The expertise was always here. There isn't one person who worked at Birds Eye who hasn't found work somewhere else.

'At Birds Eye it was family. Your mother worked there, daughters worked, everybody worked, so when the place closed down, you didn't just sit on yer laurels, you was used to working, so you went and got another job.'

As the older and more experienced members of staff retired, inevitably new arrivals changed the atmosphere at Birds Eye. When Lorraine Scott left, she went to work at Jacksons in Gypsyville.

'I loved me job at Birds Eye. I would 'ave stayed, yeah. My sister, Andrea, broke down crying when she 'ad to leave. When that place closed down our Joanne and my brother-in-law, Dave, they lost both their incomes because they both worked there. Our Joanne got a job at Home Bargains and me brother-in-law he just takes what he can now. He's been working on them cabins in London.

'I could go on Hessle Road at nine o'clock in the morning and 'cos I knew that many people down there I might not get back until two or three o'clock in the afternoon. But now I don't see a soul. And then every now and again I see the odd face pop up and think, Oh I 'aven't seen them in years.'

For Lilian Scott, there's no doubt the loss of the factory played a part in the area's decline. She remembers how the girls that used to work at Birds Eye would come to Hessle Road early to shop.

'If they was coming to start work at twelve o'clock to five they'd catch the early bus come on to Hessle Road an hour earlier, then on to work.'

Eddie Rokahr has one particular memory of his time at Birds Eye and a song that came back to haunt him when he least expected.

'It wasn't long after Radio One started up in a morning and there was one particular piece of music that came out, Judy Collins Amazing Grace. And they used to pipe music through the factory. And when that came on for some strange reason everyone joined in. And I mean everyone in the factory started singing Amazing Grace. It didn't matter how many times a day it came on they all joined in. I'll always remember that. So many different voices, but they all seemed to blend. You might get the odd voice that stood out ... I love that song.

'Our grandson, he's the only grandchild we've got, he goes to Bacon Garth Primary School in Cottingham. They did a school play. I can't remember if it was Christmas or something like that. And he stood up, and we didn't know this was going to 'appen, but he stood up in front of the whole lot with a microphone and sang Amazing Grace. There wasn't a dry eye in the school. And I just stood there.'

In 2007, Philip Harmer managed the Hull Birds Eye factory to its closure. The closure coincided with the worst floods the region had seen in a generation.

'The main reason for the closure was that factories like that have a really high fixed cost base and there wasn't sufficient volume to justify the fixed cost. In other words, if you look at all of the capacity of the business overall, it had over capacity. For instance, in Bremerhaven, which is all part of the business in Germany, they had spare capacity to take fish fingers. So they could take that volume of work straight away without any additional cost. It would just fill their factory.

'The way that the Hull factory was set up, effectively there were two sides; there's vegetable operation – predominantly it was about pea processing, which is still very much a presence for Birds Eye in the area – and other vegetables, mainly seasonal. Then we had an operation that rolled through the full year, which was the fish products. For a period I was the Manufacturing Manager of the fish building. But after that I was also Chief Engineer of the whole plant and when it finally closed I was the last General Manager.

Birds Eye factory layout at closure 2007

'When it was announced that Birds Eye was closing, the existing General Manager moved on and I picked it up for that last year to see it to closure. We still had a plan to deliver, but it was more a technical transition than anything else. People were leaving in phases. Everybody had targets in terms of production, so once they reached that target they could leave the business, but they were paid for a period after that, so they were incentivised to get the plan finished as soon as possible.

'And then we had the last pea season in the summer of 2007, which was when we had the floods. It was horrendous, just an act of nature. That was basically the end of production in the site at that time. Because of the nature of the operation for peas, the site has a huge infrastructure including a drainage system that is absolutely massive, so the last place that was ever going to flood was the Birds Eye factory. I mean the biggest drain infrastructure in the whole of this area focused on that factory. We were like an island and everywhere around the site was flooded. I had to make sure that everybody got home safely, but we couldn't get anything in or out. It devastated the crops, all the fields were flooded, but the factory itself – absolutely high and dry.'

Who was the last person out?

'Me.'

Birds Eye closed its Hessle Road plant in 2007 with the loss of 600 jobs. However, in April 2008, the company returned to the area with one of the largest pea processing plants in the world on Brighton Street Industrial Estate. The factory is able to process and freeze around 50,000 tons of peas per year during the harvest season from June to August and is operated by the temperature-controlled logistics specialists, Christian Salvesen. Once again geography plays a key role. The plant is situated in the centre of a 30-mile radius of 200 growers with peas harvested from over 24,000 acres of land in east Yorkshire and northern Lincolnshire. The plant shells, blanches and freezes them within two-and-a-half hours of picking. During the pea season, the factory operates 24-hours a day.

In reality, the decision of Birds Eye to leave Hull closed a chapter of Hessle Road's social and industrial history. Whilst there remain a few isolated fish merchants – Smales are an old-established firm still trading locally, the industrial landscape had been changing for many years. In 2011, the closure of Hull's Fish-gate auction signalled the end of a 150-year industry. Fuelled by the decline in the fishing industry and the changing demands of new housing and the need for regeneration, the area was bound to change. Janet Wilson remembers how the first phase of regeneration fundamentally altered Hessle Road with people moving to the outskirts of the city.

'The bottom half of Somerset Street was left, but the top half got pulled down so along here (Edinburgh Street) it went right to the top of Hessle Road. So everybody at that end went to Bransholme and Orchard Park. They had the chance of coming back when they built the new houses, but the land was left for ten years. In that time they'd made their own little areas so they didn't want to come back.'

Hessle Road regeneration 1970s

Eddie Rokahr moved on from Birds Eye and the food processing industry in the mid-1970s.

'What can you do? You go out and find summat else to make your bread and butter. I went into whatever paid me enough to keep me family in a home together. I'm proud to say that whatever we've got as a family I've paid for it, I've worked for it.'

After 40 years in one house, Eddie moved on as part of the regeneration programme.

'They pulled us out. It was when the floods were on and everything that was up for sale came off the market and was rented out at extortionate rates. So it took us two years to find a place. And then we eventually found this. It broke my heart (to move out of Hawthorn Avenue). There was no choice. When I was fifty-eight – I'm sixty-eight now – I took voluntary redundancy from British Gas. I'd got twenty-three years' service in so I'd got a decent pension to come and a decent redundancy shot. It was a good job was British Gas, but every third night you were on a twenty four hour call. My lads said, "Dad, you're fifty seven, fifty eight. You don't need it." So I thought, right, I'll get out.'

Eddie works part time to top up his pension.

'I've got this little job at Edinburgh Street Centre, we stack up me wages and then when summat comes up that's how we pay for it, y'know. It's life.'

In spite of having lived in the Hessle Road community for 60 years, Eddie wasn't born there and doesn't class himself as a Hessle Roader. He has strong views about the regeneration and its damaging effect.

'If you were prepared to do your share and join in, it's always been a community and unfortunately this council devastated that community when they pulled Hessle Road down.'

For Lilian Tindle, there's still the smell of the fish docks and the factories.

'If I drive down Hessle Road and I come to Daltry Street fly-over, I can always smell it just in that one area. I can smell it plain as day.'

Patricia Rudd noticed the difference in the area when she returned from living in Germany in 1976.

'I said to my Dad, "What's up with people? They don't talk to you." I can remember, before I left, your neighbours on the terrace used to come round and some of the others, they were your friends. My Dad said, "They don't trust each other now." It was when they started knocking the slums down and putting people in new houses and going into different areas.'

Patricia's mother, Jane, remembers the family having to move shortly after they'd finished paying for their house on the Boulevard.

'We had to go. They put it (the house) under compulsory purchase, but you didn't get market value like they do today, you just got ground rent. Plus, they wanted to give us a little tiny flat, but we refused it. It was a nice property, but we didn't like the area (Bransholme). Fortunately we got an exchange and moved to Burton Pidsea.

'It felt awful. That's when everything changed because you were getting strangers all over the place and you didn't know them, they didn't know you, so you had just individuals from different places you see. Some of the people were coming from what you would actually call slums, and they would move in and within three months their property again, even though it was brand new, would be called a slum. They didn't want to talk to you because you were cleaning your windows and putting clean curtains up. They thought you were posh but you weren't, you just took pride in your property. I was lucky, I did make friends. Mind you I make friends with everybody.'

Patricia Rudd finally finished with the industry when she worked at Ross Group. By then she had two children, was living in Burstwick and working nights on the production lines while her husband worked days.

'I did it for about three years, maybe more. I was there in the morning. Get them off to school, tidy up. Then I would go to bed for about four hours, get up and get the dinner ready, give them their dinners and then get myself ready and go to work.

'I used to go on my scooter; I had a little moped to go from Burstwick to Hull. One night my helmet and my keys had gone missing. I found them down the toilet. There was a lot of jealousy if you had a little bit more than anyone else and because I lived in Burstwick the women thought I was posh. They didn't like it because I was working there and I didn't come from Hull, but I did. I come from Hessle Road. One night I just had enough. I took some cigs, put them in my pocket, went into the factory, and then one of the packets had gone and I thought, Oh God, my cigs have gone out of my pocket. I asked had anyone seen them and they all said they hadn't. Well, I could see them in one of the lass's pockets and I said, "You don't smoke what I do. You've got them in your pocket, you don't smoke them." She said "Well I bought these tonight." I said, "You didn't because I bought them from last night. I buy them in a packet of two-hundred and it says on the back *multi pack, not to be sold separately."* She wouldn't have it and I couldn't get the manageress. She said she could prove it so I said, "Open the gate I'm going home. Stuff your bloody job up your arse." They were horrible. I'd had it hard enough.'

John Talbot and his family had moved to London with John taking his skills to a wet fish shop in Southgate. He might have had to bend the truth slightly.

'I rung 'em up and told 'em a few lies. I says, "Oh yeah, I've worked in a shop." I never had. They says, "Oh, come down, we'll pay your fare." And I took me wife and children down. It was only about five pounds return then, but it was still a lot of money. So I finished up got a job there with a house, real nice, Enfield we lived. It's a real nice area, better than Hessle Road, even though I liked Hessle Road. But this was a nicer for me children. We stayed there for six years, then I come back.'

On his return, John's old contacts on the docks came in useful.

'I got me wet fish shop on Bransholme market. We lived North Road off Hessle Road, Gipsyville. I was there twenty odd years at the shop. Serving the customers. It was a fish stall, that's all I know really.

'Bransholme market was the first area in Hull to be open late on a Friday night. You know the supermarkets now, they're all open now all the time; well that was the first one, they stayed open till eight o'clock at night. And you used to get people coming in who had been to work, coming in and shopping. We sold cod, haddock, plaice, just the normal fish. I still had a lot of contacts in Hull, it all come from Hull. I went back to the firms I used to work for y'see. And I'd say, "I want to buy four or five stone of haddock." You could take it and they knew I'd come back and pay. Cash deals, you know, that's all you went on.'

Bob Carlson still sees many of the people who moved away.

'Everybody knew everybody. They all went to Bransholme, but they still come back here to shop. I says to 'em, "You live in a big 'ouse but you come here to Hessle Road for yer cheap meat." All the supervisors and managers – they only live at Kirk Ella an' that so you see 'em all at bank.'

89

Originally, Marion Carlson was moved from the area as part of the regeneration programme. It wasn't a happy experience.

'My son had epilepsy when he was little, so when we was coming out of Eton Street, they put me on Orchard Park for the fresh air. I wasn't up there a year. I felt isolated, it was 'orrible. I didn't drive. I wanted to come back and I did come back. That's how I come to buy Naburn Street, where the new houses were. I was there thirty-odd years and that's where we was until the regeneration bought us out.'

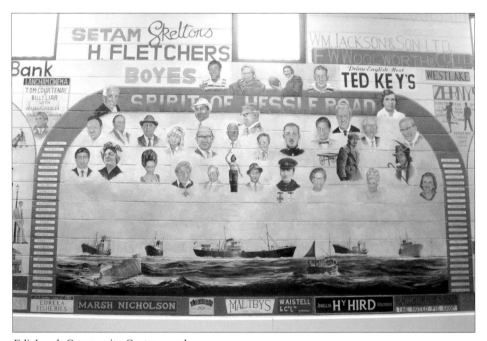

Edinburgh Community Centre mural

Marion is the Chair at the Edinburgh Street Community Centre. She has been involved there for 15 years. Her initial involvement came after the death of her daughter and the need to find something to help her grandson. She discovered a wealth of skills in community development and motivated countless others to do the same.

'Fifteen years ago I lost me daughter – and she had one boy and he was just coming up to six and I thought, I've got to get him into summat, and I took him to Edinburgh Street to start karate. But he would never let me drop him off and go home, he wanted me to stay with him. I got talking to the people

90

there, and then a lady from Hull City Council come to run it – they called her Marianne – and she said, "Would you like to come on the committee?" I said, "I don't know nowt about committees, I always worked in factories."

'She helped us learn how to get people off the street into the centre. You never saw any youths in that centre; karate they had bains in, but you never saw youths off the street. When I come to be chair in there I went round the streets 'cos I knew 'em all. I knew all the rogues – we were living there! And I said, "Why don't you come in? There's free coffee for yer." Anyhow they did come in. Don't get me wrong, they went wild. They took the phone off the wall, they did trash the place a bit … If they misbehaved I used to hit 'em with a bleedin' mop. You had to stand up to them, you couldn't be cowerin' below 'em. And I'd speak to each and every one of 'em. And we got table tennis, pool tables, we got everything, games – and d'you know they did respect the place. They'd just never been invited in. When they did come in, the elderly were sayin', "Get them bastards out."

'The old people didn't talk to me, but a community centre's for everyone. There was two youths – I'll always remember, they was eighteen – and they'd popped in for a coffee and they said, "What's going on in there?" I said, "It's bingo." They said, "Can we play?" I said, "Bingo's for anybody, long as you're eighteen." They went in, paid for their books, sat down. And the old people wouldn't start the game while them went. So I had to ask the lads to come into the pop-in where you have cups of tea and I said, "This isn't the place for you if that's how they want to carry on. You've still got your own nights." They was fine. They had that much respect, but the elderly didn't want 'em in that centre.

'That's changed now, hundred per-cent it's changed. I mean the lads that came to karate, they're bringing their own bains now. There's another generation coming through. Even now some of them youths, if they need a passport, they'll come to me and I'll sign the forms. When they've been up at court I've wrote letters after letters saying what good lads they are now to what they was.'

With the fishermen's mural on the walls of the centre, Edinburgh Street is a well-established hub for activities within the Hessle Road community. The centre supports mother and toddler groups, mothers with children who have behavioural difficulties and continues to provide activities for younger and older people in the community.

'The OAPs have had two lots of trips this year, Skegness and Whitby. At Christmas, we cater for up to a hundred people for a Christmas day in the centre.

We pay for an artist, we pay for all the food, a full day of everything and we get cake at Christmas. This is for people who might be on their own Christmas day. I went door knocking in the snow to get 'em in. I'll always remember this chap, I knocked and he opened the door as though he was keepin' 'isself back, and I explained we was doin' a Christmas party for them who's vulnerable, in their house, who don't see anybody. He said, "But I've never been in the centre." I said, "Well come in the centre. Come in and have a cup of tea: if you don't want to come to the Christmas drop in an 'ave a cup of tea." And it's the best thing he's ever done, he comes in two or three times a week, just from me knocking on his door.

'We've got the bingo going now and they come from Glasgow Street, Gypsyville, 'cos it gets around and we don't charge for going in. It's a community centre.'

It's important for Marion and those who work and volunteer at Edinburgh Street that something of the spirit of Hessle Road is preserved. The centre is a meeting place for people and a focus for local councillors, the police and the latest regeneration scheme. There's no doubting Marion's affinity with the area and its people.

'If I won the lottery tomorrow I'd never move off Hessle Road. Never. I was born on Hessle Road. If I won a thousand million I wouldn't move, I wouldn't.'

What would Marion do with a lottery win?

'I'd 'elp everybody's who's helped me.'

*

*In the final stages of putting the Pattie Slappers book together, we received the sad news that Marion Carlson had died suddenly. She was an enthusiastic contributor to the project, a spirited community activist and a proud Hessle Roader who will be missed by all who knew her. The extracts from her interviews are published here with the kind permission of Marion's husband, Bob Carlson.*

# Acknowledgements

We would like to thank: Heritage Lottery Fund for their support; CERT Ltd – Neil King, Chris Mason, Rick Keightley and staff; Birds Eye – Phil Harmer, Brian Wheatley; Hull History Centre; The Carnegie Heritage Centre, Hull – Sheila Coates; St. Andrews Dock Heritage Park Action Group (STAND) – Anita Waddy; Edinburgh Street Community Centre – Simon Pickering, Janet Wilson, Pearl Anderson, George Magee; Hull Daily Mail; Yorkshire Film Archive and BBC Radio Humberside, particularly David Burns, Helen Scholefield, James Hoggarth and Kate Murphy.

Special thanks to Pearl Anderson, Mike Edenbrow, Judy Galloway, Mike Galloway, Neil King and Lilian Tindle for volunteering to proof read the draft of Pattie Slappers.

Thanks to the following for donation of photographs: Marion Carlson, Gerry Raines, Eddy Rokahr, Patricia Rudd, Rosanne Wilding, Janet Wilson, Jose Verbist, Birds Eye, Hull Daily Mail and Yorkshire Film Archive

Most importantly, we would offer sincere thanks to the following who came forward, gave us their time and trusted us to tell their story:

**Interviewees**

Pearl Anderson

Philip Bunting

Bob Carlson

Marion Carlson

Bob Carver

Ivy Gallagher

Mike Galloway

Judy Galloway

Bill Garton

Jackie Gower

Margaret Green

Philip Harmer

Neil King

Beatty Lee

George Magee

Gerry Raines

Eddie Rokahr

Karen Rouse-Dean

Jane Rudd

Patricia Rudd

Lilian Scott

Lorraine Scott

John Talbot

Lilian Tindle

Jose Verbist

Janet Wilson

# Bibliography

**Publications:**

A Little Bird – Birds Eye Hull internal newsletter, Edition 9, June 1978
Birds Eye and the UK Frozen Food Industry – Robert M. Grant
Birds Eye Employee Handbook – Unilever Organization, circa 1970s
Distant Water – Nick Triplow, Tina Bramhill, Sophie James, North Wall Publishing, 2011
Good Old Hessle Road – Alec Gill, Hutton Press 1991
Herring Women – Karen Foy, Ancestors Magazine, Issue 56, March 2007
Hull Daily Mail – various articles: July 28, 2012; May 11, June 21, 2011; May 27, December 10, 2009; 24 June, 2008
The Spirit of Hessle Road – Characters featured at the Edinburgh Street Community Centre, Edinburgh Street, 2012
The Women They Left Behind – Nick Triplow, Tina Bramhill, Jade Shepherd, Fathom Press 2009


**Websites:**

www.celtic-seafoods.co.uk
www.birdseye.com
www.findusgroup.com
www.hullfair.net
www.hullfishingheritage.org.uk
www.hullwebs.co.uk
www.paul-gibson.com
www.vitalfootball.co.uk
www.yorkshirepride.co.uk


**Unpublished sources:**

Fish dock memories – Mike Galloway
Bobbers – John Talbot
Memories of Percy and Ethel Saul – Kathleen May Scotney, nee Saul. Kindly donated by Rosanne Wilding
Birds Eye Employee memorabilia – Jose Verbist
Personal memories of working in Hessle Road Co-op – Maureen Hurren-Richardson

# About the author

Nick Triplow is a freelance writer, editor and teacher. Born in London and now living in Barton upon Humber, Nick is the author of: Distant Water – Stories from Grimsby's Fishing Industry; The Women They Left Behind – Stories from Grimsby's Fishing Families; Family Ties – Stories from Hall's Barton Ropery. He has published several pieces of short fiction and his debut novel Frank's Wild Years was published by Caffeine Nights in 2012. Nick also co-wrote the script for Ted's Return Home, a short film about Ted Lewis, author of the novel Get Carter, as well as contributing to Lewis's Return Home, a BBC Radio 4 documentary about Lewis. He is currently finishing his biography of Lewis and working on other writing projects.